Young**Writers**

2004 POETR

ONCE
A RHYME

IMAGINATION FOR
A NEW GENERATION

Poems From The
West Country

Edited by Lynsey Hawkins

 Young**Writers**

First published in Great Britain in 2005 by:
Young Writers
Remus House
Coltsfoot Drive
Peterborough
PE2 9JX
Telephone: 01733 890066
Website: www.youngwriters.co.uk

SB ISBN 1 84460 664 3

Foreword

Young Writers was established in 1991 and has been passionately devoted to the promotion of reading and writing in children and young adults ever since. The quest continues today. Young Writers remains as committed to engendering the fostering of burgeoning poetic and literary talent as ever.

This year's Young Writers competition has proven as vibrant and dynamic as ever and we are delighted to present a showcase of the best poetry from across the UK. Each poem has been carefully selected from a wealth of *Once Upon A Rhyme* entries before ultimately being published in this, our twelfth primary school poetry series.

Once again, we have been supremely impressed by the overall high quality of the entries we have received. The imagination, energy and creativity which has gone into each young writer's entry made choosing the best poems a challenging and often difficult but ultimately hugely rewarding task - the general high standard of the work submitted amply vindicating this opportunity to bring their poetry to a larger appreciative audience.

We sincerely hope you are pleased with our final selection and that you will enjoy *Once Upon A Rhyme Poems From The West Country* for many years to come.

Contents

Michael Poat (9)   1

Air Balloon Hill Junior School, Bristol
Jenna Harvey (8)   1
Amy Rowlands (9)   2
Charlotte Dent (9)   3
Zainab Halepota (9)   4

Ashleworth CE Primary School, Ashleworth
Olivia Raine (8)   4
Elisabeth Fish (10)   5
Sophie Aspey-Smith (8)   5
Chelsea Cooper (9)   6
Rhianne Huggins (10)   6
Amelia Jones (9)   7
Zack Miller (9)   7
Samantha Finch (8)   8
Robert Taylor Clark (9)   9
Ryan Sheppard (9)   9
Ruth Sumner (11)   9
Bethany Hughes (11)   10
Harry Cook (10)   10
Oliver Mansfield (9)   11

Bishops Sutton Primary School, Bishops Sutton
Patrick Fenton (10)   11
Ellie Salt (9)   12

Brimscombe CE Primary School, Stroud
Andrew Dipple (7)   12
Jack Stonham (8)   12
Fiachna O'Brien (7)   13
Rebekah Jones (7)   13
Charlotte Dalby (7)   13
Gabriel O'Regan (8)   14
Brodie Dart (8)   14
Henry Kemp (8)   14

Harry Leeming (7)   15
Stanley Howlett (7)   15
Tia Dean (7)   15
Anna Kingston (8)   16
Georgia Dixon (8)   16
Tyler Stevens (8)   17
Callum House (7)   17
Timothy Yates Round (8)   17
Jenny Wells (8)   18
Gemma Hone (8)   18
Nicholas Boden (8)   18
Travis Law (8)   19
Joe Hayden (8)   19
Thomas Stevens (8)   19

Coniston Primary School, Bristol
Jacob Houghton (10)   20
David Dunnings (10)   21
Leigh Bevan (10)   21
Daniel Mann (10)   22

Croft Primary School, Painswick
Emily Dowdeswell (10)   22
Lydia Thornton (10)   23
Kyle Douglass (10)   23
Cressida Mawdesley-Thomas (10)   24
Evangeline Edgworth (10)   24
Alicia Barnett (10)   25
Felix Gilding (11)   25
Stephanie Jones (10)   26
Robert Sidwell (10)   26
Abigail Garbett (10)   26
Benjamin Pigott (10)   27
Henry Jackson (10)   27
Tamara Manton (10)   27
Rebecca Elliott (10)   28
Rosemary Davies (11)   28
Kyle Douglass (10)   28
William Jackson (10)   29
Samuel Andrews (10)   29
William Moir (10)   29

Farrington Gurney CE Primary School, Bristol

Marley Hall (9)	30
Lauren Thompson (11)	30
Hugh Jefferey (9)	31
Tom Horman (9)	31
Tom Plummer (10)	32
Kirsty Jones (10)	33
Jack Gianella (10)	33
Ben Taylor (10)	34
Emma Jones (9)	34
Lucy Elliott (9)	35
Jordan Malkin (10)	35

Frenchay CE Primary School, Bristol

Amy Hillier (9)	35
Lucy Quantick (9)	36
Andrew Smith (9)	36
Daniel Kembery (9)	37
Ella Hayden (9)	37
Claire Ali (10)	37
Laura Brown (10)	38
Lily Grant (8)	38
Georgia Maxwell (9)	38
Ella Pullin (7)	39
Jemma Kinsey (10)	40

Kempsford CE (VC) Primary School, Kempsford

Ella Williams (8)	40
David Mather (9)	41
Daragh Smith (9)	41
Emily Hepworth (9)	41
CanJarri McKinley (8)	42
Callum Cornish (8)	42
Connor Denness (8)	42
Thomas Windsor (8)	43
Ellie Wrona (9)	43
Kristy Britt (9)	44
Emily Guthrie (9)	44
Lacey Moulden (9)	45
Emily Dixon-Fallon (10)	45
Sarah White (10)	45

George Irving (10)	46
Annabel Stagg (8)	46
Ellie Maundrell (7)	47
Sophie Cornish (11)	47
Joseph Housley (9)	48
Nicola Axel-Berg (7)	48
Lucy Gray (9)	48
Beth Hallam (9)	49
David Caswell (10)	49
Holly Strange (9)	49
Alice Green (7)	50
Amy Russell (10)	50
Thomas Hallam (10)	50
Joseph James (9)	51

Norton Primary School, Gloucester

Jordan Bryan (10)	51
Rhys Baird (10)	51
Amy Spiers (9)	52
Sam Steel (9)	52
Marykate Bowers (10)	52
Rosie Evans (9)	52
Chantelle Packman (9)	53
Lucy Jones (10)	53
Laurence Anscombe (9)	53
Jack Steel (11)	54
Ryan Merry (10)	54
Mark Kerry (10)	55
Emily Stagg (10)	55
Charlotte Smith (10)	56
Erica Webb (10)	56
Carys Owen (9)	57

Portishead Primary School, Portishead

Siân Whitehorn (8)	57
Thomas Clark (8)	58
Charlotte Clements (7)	58
Ella Whittle (8)	58
Jess Burns (8)	59
Poppy Manning (8)	59
Freya Park (8)	60

Olivia Pointon (8)   61
Joel Hopkins (8)   61
Thomas Kimberley (8)   62
Emily Wall (8)   62
William Instance (8)   62

Raysfield Junior School, Chipping Sodbury

Ellie Smith (9)	63
Adam Turton (9)	63
Cameron Hector (9)	64
Katie Hooper (9)	64
Alex McMillan (9)	65
Mitchell Evans (9)	65
Natasha Kilbane (9)	66
Rebecca Biggs (9)	67
Harriet Dean (9)	68
Ben Weaver (9)	69

Tibberton Community Primary School, Tibberton

Katie Davies (8)	69
Tom Heathfield (8)	70
Oliver Beale (9)	70
Wednesday Batchelor (10)	71
Catherine Goodwin (9)	71
Abigail Pearce (7)	72
Callum Hall (10)	72
Declan Beale (7)	72

Warden Hill Primary School, Cheltenham

David Burns (9)	73
Oliver Blay (9)	73
Jake Heath (10)	73
Lauren Lewis (9)	74
Jack Kelly (10)	74
Hannah Martin (9)	74
Adam Dunlop (9)	75
James Kear (9)	75
Jamie Todd (9)	75
Holly Isherwood (9)	76
Jonathan Rosagro (9)	76
Harvey Phelps (10)	76

Ben Harris (10)	77
Elena Ferro Kirby (9)	77
Ahbab Rahman (9)	77
Selina Islam (10)	78
Ellie Pitt (9)	78
Ryan Wiggett-Parker (10)	78
Heather Didcote (9)	79
Elayna Cambridge (9)	79
Kaye Pollard (9)	79
Holly Smith (9)	80
Samantha Rawlings (10)	80
Sam Wedley (9)	80
Matt Street (9)	81
Romillie Compton (9)	81
Matthew Barnfield (9)	81
Adam Hannis (9)	82
Millie Dawson (9)	82
Billy Wright (9)	82
Tom Williams (9)	83
Ellen Pearce (9)	83
Matthew Armitage (9)	83
Daniel Jacques (9)	84
Joe Williams (9)	84
Jodie Cave (9)	84
Harriet Oddy (9)	85
Rebecca Faull (9)	85
Thomas Hayward (9)	85
Iain Greig (9)	86
Sam Godwin (9)	86
Cheryl Davies (9)	86
Rachael Carruthers (9)	87
Sam Holdaway (9)	87
Jake Rostron (9)	87
Poppie Compton (9)	88
Natasha Goodwin (9)	88
Lauren Greville (9)	88

Westbury Park Primary School, Bristol

Hannah Jones (8)	89
Jessica Bell (8)	89
Hannah Brindle (8)	90

Cecily Bain (8)	90
Abigael Brain (8)	90
Fleur Sainsbury (10)	91
Isabel Avery (8)	91
Lauren Cuttell (8)	91
Ella Jones (8)	92
Celia Johnson-Morgan (8)	92
Kamarl Rauf (8)	93
Emily Bull (8)	93
Jocelyn Eccles (8)	93
Flora Jetha (8)	94
Lois Barton (8)	94
Emily Staricoff (8)	94
Jasmine Taylor (11)	95
Monica Lindsay-Perez (8)	95
Safiya Bashir (10)	96
Rachel Bews (8)	96
Natalie Oxford & Charlotte Moran (10)	97
Clemency Carroll (8)	97
Zoe Rasbash (8)	98
Millie Snook (11)	99
Thomas Hellin (10)	99
Tilly Maidment-Otlet (10)	100
Jessie Moran (8)	100
Elsa Andreski (10)	101
Daniel Cullum (8)	101
Esmé Bain (11)	102
Sean Jamshidi (11)	103
Nicola Papastavrou Brooks (10)	104
Rose Ireland (11)	104
Georgie Hope (10)	105
Jade Hellin (10)	105
Alice Dale (10)	106
Tom Last (9)	106

West Town Lane Junior School, Brislington

Emily Jennings & Rianna Newman (8)	107
Kayleigh Sims (8)	107
Michael Dyer (10)	108
Ashley Lewis (8)	109
Adrienne Day (9)	110

Lauren Payne (8) 110
Conner Neale (10) 111
Daisy Pearce-Lyons (8) 111
Chloe Little (8) 112
Samantha Jones (10) 112
Grace Haines (10) 113
Abby Hoyle (10) 113
Emma Brown (10) 114
Conor Woods (8) 114
Laura McEllin (11) 115
Isabella Broome (9) 115
Daniel Griffin (10) 116
Jack Rogers (11) 116
Lydia Hughes (8) 117
Jack Bostock (10) 117
Daisy Jones (10) 118
Liam Plumpton (11) 118
Bethany Cooper (10) 119
Thomas Edwards (10) 119
Tom Payne (10) 120
Alice Gregory (10) 120
Eleanor Baldock (10) 121
Matthew Flook (10) 121
Chloe Jenkins (10) 122
Dino Carobene (10) 123
Corrie Rose (10) 124
Jessica Randall (9) 125
Sian Purnell (10) 126
Sam Hanks (10) 126
Hannah Cheung (10) 127
Bradley Meaker (10) 128
Joshua Hughes (10) 129
Joshua Woodman (10) 130
Bethany Newman (10) 131
Sophie Tatum (10) 132
Kirsty Whatling & Emily Bourne (10) ... 133

The Poems

Swimming

Swimming is my favourite sport,
It really keeps me fit,
My favourite stroke is butterfly,
I am quite good at it!

When I've got my flippers on,
I really go quite fast,
The whistle blows, we're off - a race,
I don't want to be last!

Now it's time for ten lengths front crawl.
'Off you go, chop, chop.'
I'm off as fast as a bullet.
'Go on, heads down, don't stop!'

Now is the end of the lesson,
I really am exhausted,
I am off to get changed,
Then off home to my bed!

Michael Poat (9)

Dancing Ballerinas

Up on tiptoe all about
Jump here, jump over there -
Turn around, skip around
That's it, gently turn again
That's a lovely time
Dancing around, jumping and hopping
Turning around and give applause
And that's the end of the show!

Jenna Harvey (8)
Air Balloon Hill Junior School, Bristol

Winter Days

Monday:
>The hurricane comes and the first snowflakes fall
>a touch of frost reaches the shimmering lake
>and no more is it water, it's icy cold
>the sun is bold and there is nothing left of summer

Tuesday:
>Not much green left on the planet of life
>no green, no orange, no brown, all the colours
>matching white, white, just white, white, white
>white as a dove, with snow all over, whiter than
>>you could imagine

Wednesday:
>The hurricane of winter has come, the trees have
>died and nothing is coloured anymore
>all the colours have been sucked up from the
>planet of life and it has become all the same colour

Thursday:
>The grass has turned the snow, the ponds of water
>have turned to a pond of ice, all the trees have
>become frozen hands coming out from
>the ground, the Earth has become a ball of ice

Friday:
>Then I just go out and play in the snow
>it's cold, cold, cold, freezing cold, so don't forget
>to dress up warmly, scarf, gloves, coat and hat
>and just inside a body warmer

Saturday:
>Then it's night, a blustery night, snowflakes falling
>everywhere but you're all snug in your bed
>or probably sat by the fire on a rug
>whatever you do, at least you're warm

Sunday:

>At the end of the week the storm starts to go
>and at last you can see the sun, the blue sky
>and the bluebirds tweet and flowers come out of the
>ground but then you say, 'I can't wait 'til next winter'
>but then I think, *it's not over yet*
>it happens every year.

Amy Rowlands (9)
Air Balloon Hill Junior School, Bristol

Seasons Change

Autumn days,
autumn days have come,
but we still have some sun.
Leaves are falling off the trees,
in the blustery autumn breeze.

Red, yellow, green and brown,
leaves are falling from the ground.
Hats and coats we have to wear,
because of the autumn air.

Squirrels scurry in the ground,
searching for the nuts they found.
Hedgehogs hibernate in the leaves,
because they cannot climb the trees.

Spring days,
sunflowers sprouting out of the ground,
poppies and daisies all around.
Buds burst open with new lives,
the grass is green, so are the chives.

Scarlet-red, lilac-blue,
flowers blooming, 'I'll pick some for you!'
The weather's warmer, so's your smile,
spending time in spring is so worthwhile.

Charlotte Dent (9)
Air Balloon Hill Junior School, Bristol

Summer In The Country

Roses scarlet, smelling sweet,
Clusters of fresh corn and wheat,
Emerald grass and flowers gold,
Sun is shining, sun is bold.

Summer's breath is in the air,
Butterflies dance without a care,
Stretching your face into a smile,
The flowers go on for quite a mile!

Sunshine giggles at the trees,
I hear the hum of honeybees,
The poppies red, the daisies white,
They're a rather pretty sight!

Now as the day begins to fade,
The sky turns a reddish shade,
Then the night begins to fall,
The day has ended after all.

Zainab Halepota (9)
Air Balloon Hill Junior School, Bristol

Dogs

Big dogs, little dogs.
Good dogs, bad dogs.
Floppy ears, pointy ears.
Fat dogs, thin dogs.
Ugly dogs, cute dogs.
Sharp teeth, blunt teeth.
Tinned food, dry food.
Happy dogs, sad dogs.
Some dogs live in streets, other in houses.
Dogs are the cutest animals on Earth!

Olivia Raine (8)
Ashleworth CE Primary School, Ashleworth

The Way Of The World

Clocks go 'purr purr,'
fans go 'roar!'

Roses smell of cabbages
and pots arrange marriages.

Cupboards go 'quack quack'
kettles go 'glub'

Lilies smell of rotting fish
so if I had a final wish

It would have to be this
to make everything go back to how it really is.

So . . .

Clocks go 'tick-tock'
fans go 'whirr'

Cupboards go 'open, close'
kettles go 'hiss'

And I'd like the world to stay like this!

Elisabeth Fish (10)
Ashleworth CE Primary School, Ashleworth

It Was A Dark, Dark Night

It was a dark, dark night
And the stars were shining bright
It was the end of the day
So the moon came out to play
And the children were asleep in their beds
And the bats were flattering the leaves in the trees
So that was the dark, dark night.

Sophie Aspey-Smith (8)
Ashleworth CE Primary School, Ashleworth

Seasons

Feel the fresh spring where the new animals are born.
Feel the fresh spring where the yellow daffodils grow.
Feel the fresh spring where the children come out to play.
Feel the fresh spring where the wet dew is on the green grass.
Feel the fresh spring where the Easter bunny gives
                              children Easter eggs.

Feel the hot summer where the sun comes out to play.
Feel the hot summer where children enjoy their summer holidays.
Feel the hot summer where the sky is bright blue.
Feel the hot summer where the sun shines up at you.
Feel the hot summer where the birds sing in the summer sun.

Feel the cold autumn where the children watch the brown leaves fall.
Feel the cold autumn where the children collect the falling conkers.
Feel the cold autumn where the children watch the beautiful
                              fireworks on Guy Fawkes' night.
Feel the cold autumn where the children dress up and
                              celebrate Hallowe'en.
Feel the cold autumn where the children pick the juicy blackberries.

Feel the frozen winter where everybody celebrates Christmas.
Feel the frozen winter where the children make snowmen.
Feel the frozen winter where we have a happy new year.
Feel the frozen winter where the snowflakes fall on your nose.

Chelsea Cooper (9)
Ashleworth CE Primary School, Ashleworth

Rainbow

Red is from the fire of a green scaled dragon.
Orange is from the boiling hot sun in a heat wave.
Yellow is from the most sour lemon that anyone's ever tasted.
Green is from a piece of grass from the deepest darkest forest.
Blue is from the sky on a fresh summer's day.
Indigo is from the first plum that drops.
Violet is from the lavender that makes your hands smell nice.

Rhianne Huggins (10)
Ashleworth CE Primary School, Ashleworth

In The Jungle

As you climb through the big leaves,
In the blistering heat,
You might see a monkey swing,
Or even a tiger leap.

You could hear an elephant walking,
Or a parrot squawking,
You could taste the yummy oranges,
Sprouting above your head.

You could feel the distant breeze,
Blowing in your hair,
The exciting movement
Everywhere.

Then you turn around and see
The animals,
I wonder what they think
Of *me?*

Amelia Jones (9)
Ashleworth CE Primary School, Ashleworth

Ninjas

Ninjas are good and some are bad,
they're always happy and they're never sad.

Ninjas are mean and ninjas are keen
and they don't like to eat their greens.

Ninjas wear black
and they're fast like a cat.

Ninjas are warriors from ancient Japan
and I'm a great fan!

Zack Miller (9)
Ashleworth CE Primary School, Ashleworth

Faces

Sad face,
Happy face,
Never show an angry face.

Baby face,
Wrinkly face,
Always tell a story face.

White face,
Black face,
All the colours of the world face.

Friendly face,
Foe face,
Wanted to be loved face.

Freckle face,
Spotty face,
Not just a pretty face.

Fat face,
Thin face,
Doesn't matter which face.

Clean face,
Dirty face,
Enjoying having fun face.

Puzzled face,
Blank face,
Always on the move face.

Rich face,
Poor face,
Every face is a beautiful face!

Samantha Finch (8)
Ashleworth CE Primary School, Ashleworth

Squirrel Act

He scurries quickly like a grey flash,
If you scare him he will dash,
His tail up high, he hops along walls,
The nuts he chooses look rather like green balls.

He balances well on twigs and branches,
He leaps from bough to bough,
Gnawing green skin off nuts,
Scaling carefully up leafy heights.

With nuts in his mouth, he sits staring,
His body hunched, brown eyes glaring,
Once he's reaped his nutty harvest
And berries mixed in too,
He stores it away
And sleeps the winter through.

Robert Taylor Clark (9)
Ashleworth CE Primary School, Ashleworth

Feelings

They are like a rainbow
They taste like love
They look like a dove
They are like angels
They feel like happiness.

Ryan Sheppard (9)
Ashleworth CE Primary School, Ashleworth

Fairytale

Dance along to the fairy beat,
Wave your wand and tap your feet,
Dance along as the fairies play,
Point your toes and fly away.

Ruth Sumner (11)
Ashleworth CE Primary School, Ashleworth

My Fairy Friend

I have a fairy friend,
Who drives me round the bend.
Her name is Lilly,
She's very silly,
I'm her bestest friend.

She's got baby cheeks
And eyes green as leeks.
Silky hair that's very fair,
Her lips are smooth and very pink,
When she sees me, she gives me a wink.

Her dress is made of a red, red rose
And white shoes that cover up her toes.
Her house is made of a walnut shell,
On her door there is a bell.

She lives in my tree
And she loves me.

Bethany Hughes (11)
Ashleworth CE Primary School, Ashleworth

Bonfire Night

Time to wrap up nice and cosy,
Faces are bright and cheeks are rosy.
Light the bonfire, stand very still,
Seems so exciting, until . . .

Whizz, bang, crackle, pop,
Will this noise ever stop?
Blue, red, yellow, green,
The brightest fireworks you've ever seen.

Pretty colours light up the sky,
I hope no aeroplanes are flying by.
Please remember to stay safe everyone,
Let's not spoil our Bonfire Night fun.

Harry Cook (10)
Ashleworth CE Primary School, Ashleworth

Rugby

Rugby is a tough old game
I love to play it just the same
Rucks and mauls and line-out calls
Scrums and tries and odd-shaped balls

Whatever the weather, cold and wet
I'll be out there playing, just you bet!
So rugby is the game I play
From September through till May.

Oliver Mansfield (9)
Ashleworth CE Primary School, Ashleworth

The World Is Turning Slowly

The world is turning slowly
In a very boring way
There's nothing very interesting
It's a very boring day

Football's lost its players
Sailing's lost its boat
The stupid farmer who lives next door
He's just lost his goat

The roller coaster's broken down
The bumpers have gone too
And unfortunately for me, not for them
The animals have escaped from the zoo!

The widescreen TV has just broken
The telephone wire's just blown
My best friend's house just suddenly collapsed
So that leaves me left on my own

The world is turning slowly
In a very boring way
There's nothing very interesting
It's a very boring day!

Patrick Fenton (10)
Bishops Sutton Primary School, Bishops Sutton

He's Coming . . .

He's coming . . .
Closer, closer,
Walking, stalking.
On the hill top,
Watching, waiting.
Just standing there,
Staring, searching,
Crash!
He's falling, falling,
Bumping, bumping,
Silence . . .

Ellie Salt (9)
Bishops Sutton Primary School, Bishops Sutton

Happiness

Happiness is gold like a shiny coin.
It smells like a barbecue.
It looks like a party.
It sounds like people laughing.
It feels like money in my pocket.
It reminds me of green wobbly jelly.

Andrew Dipple (7)
Brimscombe CE Primary School, Stroud

Fun

Fun is shiny bright gold like the gleaming, glowing Queen's jewels.
It sounds like an orchestra playing in London.
It reminds me of when I was a baby.
It tastes like chocolate and vanilla ice cream after dinner.
It looks like an Xbox and TV come to life.
It feels like my three furry kittens.

Jack Stonham (8)
Brimscombe CE Primary School, Stroud

Sadness

Sadness is so grey and gloomy
It makes me want to cry
It tastes like bitter chick peas from the compost
It smells like salty tears
It looks like melting honey from the cauldron
It sounds like sizzling batter in the frying pan
It feels like a burning ball that you can't get out
It reminds me of my sister crying.

Fiachna O'Brien (7)
Brimscombe CE Primary School, Stroud

Happiness

Happiness is a sparkling golden colour of the sun.
It smells like yummy chocolate in the sweet shop.
It tastes like fish and chips at the seaside.
It feels like soft fluffy cotton wool-like clouds.
It sounds like soft gentle music.
It reminds me of my best present I got for Christmas.

Rebekah Jones (7)
Brimscombe CE Primary School, Stroud

Happiness

Happiness is gold like the hot sun.
It tastes like a yellow lemon.
It sounds like a song thrush singing
It smells like fish and chips cooking in the oven.
It reminds me of my Uncle Paul and Auntie Fiona's wedding.
It looks like a gold crown shining in the sun.
It feels like a necklace of colourful beads.

Charlotte Dalby (7)
Brimscombe CE Primary School, Stroud

Fun

Fun is shiny bright gold
like the gleaming, glowing jewels.
It tastes like sticky toffee pudding.
It smells like popcorn being made at the cinema.
It sounds like a fairground ride
playing a happy tune.
It reminds me of a sunny, sandy beach
with a blue sky.
It feels like a soft velvet blanket.
It looks like a magnificent golden
eagle flying high up in the sky.

Gabriel O'Regan (8)
Brimscombe CE Primary School, Stroud

Hate

Hate is glowing orange and like lava boiling and bubbling.
It smells like burning toast or plastic being thrown into a furnace
of flames and melting like chocolate.
It tastes like hot chilli and a bad stew that's mouldy and runny.
It feels like a twister in your head swirling round and round.
It looks like an annoying elf playing around your legs.
It sounds like a kettle whining and whining.
It reminds me of my brother in Toys 'R' Us.

Brodie Dart (8)
Brimscombe CE Primary School, Stroud

Anger

Anger is red like a fierce dragon.
It smells like snails.
It sounds like my mum stamping.
It feels like burning hot lava.
It reminds me of my annoying sister.
It tastes like a horrible lizard soup.

Henry Kemp (8)
Brimscombe CE Primary School, Stroud

Happiness

Happiness is blue
Like the sea waving from side to side
It looks like fudge ice cream
It tastes like chocolate
It feels like laughter
It reminds me of Christmas
It smells like fresh air.

Harry Leeming (7)
Brimscombe CE Primary School, Stroud

Sadness

Sadness is satin blue.
Sadness tastes like a grain of salt.
Sadness feels like a wet tissue.
Sadness smells like a bit of frost.
Sadness sounds like the wind howling.
Sadness reminds me of the dentist pulling my tooth out.

Stanley Howlett (7)
Brimscombe CE Primary School, Stroud

Happiness

Happiness is a shiny penny
It reminds me of the tree moving from side to side in the distance
It sounds like the children splashing in the sea
It tastes like the salt off the fish and chips
It smells like the rose in my garden
It feels like the sun shining upon me.

Tia Dean (7)
Brimscombe CE Primary School, Stroud

Happiness

Happiness is silver like a peaceful flower
Slowly opening in the breeze.
It sounds like the trees swaying
From side to side in the distance.
It tastes like creamy chocolate in your mouth.
It smells like the smell of fish and chips
Coming towards you.
It feels like a peaceful breeze
It's making me fall asleep.
It looks like a bunch of flowers
In the supermarket.
It reminds me of when I went
On a cycle velo on holiday.

Anna Kingston (8)
Brimscombe CE Primary School, Stroud

Hate

Hate is red and black
like burning flames.
It tastes like stinging nettles
stinging my mouth.
It sounds like thunder
rumbling through the sky.
It feels like an oven
burning my fingers, sizzling my skin.
It looks like people
fighting each other.
It reminds me of red-hot lava
spilling over the volcano.

Georgia Dixon (8)
Brimscombe CE Primary School, Stroud

Fun

Fun is shiny bright gold like the
gleaming, glowing diamonds.
It looks like golden people
playing in the park.
It sounds like a great big party.
It reminds me of my cute
cuddly little dog.
It tastes like sweet apple pie.
It feels like a small soft cushion.

Tyler Stevens (8)
Brimscombe CE Primary School, Stroud

Sadness

Sadness is grey like gloomy mist in the salty sky.
It sounds like a vicious hurricane whirling in my head.
It feels like scalding hot volcanic lava as soon as the volcano's
erupted.
It tastes like rotten apple peel.

Callum House (7)
Brimscombe CE Primary School, Stroud

Hate

Hate is pitch-black like dark clouds.
It sounds like a dark bomb blowing up.
It feels like a strong rattle in my head.
It looks like a black fierce bull charging.
It smells like a smelly, raw fish.
It reminds me of destruction and death.

Timothy Yates Round (8)
Brimscombe CE Primary School, Stroud

Hate

Hate is red with flames like boiling hot lava
Spilling over the side of the volcano.
It tastes like wild, bitter berries and strong onions.
It sounds like screaming from a baby
Going through your head.
It reminds me of when Jack died, I hated it.
It looks black with little lights.
It smells like mouldy coleslaw
Festering in the fridge.
It feels like me getting bullied,
Lonely and frightened.

Jenny Wells (8)
Brimscombe CE Primary School, Stroud

Anger

Anger is red and black like a crazy baboon.
It looks like a fierce flood.
It sounds like a thunderstorm getting me all wet.
It feels like horrible, rough skin.
It tastes like my mum shouting at me.
It reminds me of my dog and my squeaky guinea pig.
It smells like rotten eggs boiling in the oven.

Gemma Hone (8)
Brimscombe CE Primary School, Stroud

Hate

Hate is like an ugly, fat pig rolling in mud.
It feels being like selfish and not liking others.
It sounds like waves crashing into people's hearts.
It tastes like rotten apples.
It smells like damp drains.
Its colour is like pitch-black.

Nicholas Boden (8)
Brimscombe CE Primary School, Stroud

Darkness

Darkness is pitch-black like the night sky
Darkness looks like me falling asleep
Darkness tastes like dirt, real dirt
Darkness sounds like one million drums in my head
Darkness feels like being beaten up.

Travis Law (8)
Brimscombe CE Primary School, Stroud

Hate

Hate is boiling hot, red like lava
It looks like a big bomb exploding
It smells like a disgusting stink bomb
It tastes like sour berries
It sounds like the scream of a baby
It feels like your blood boiling
It reminds me of my brother bullying me.

Joe Hayden (8)
Brimscombe CE Primary School, Stroud

Anger

Anger is red like lava,
It looks like a tornado going around and around,
It smells like the salty sea at the beach,
It feels like dry mud and wet mud,
It reminds me of my dad and mum,
It tastes like strong pepper.

Thomas Stevens (8)
Brimscombe CE Primary School, Stroud

Cast Out, Cast Out

Stones at your feet
The tide coming fast
Quickly get to the boat
And tighten the mast
Quickly set sail
Or we'll have to bail

Cast out, cast out
With a six ounce lead
Cast out, cast out
Don't hit me on the head

Look at that fish
Quick, try and catch it
Don't cast too hard
You'll miss with a hit
You caught one that weighs
Eight pounds and ten
Looks like we're having
Fish for tea then

Don't cast out, don't cast out
With that six ounce lead
Don't cast out, don't cast out
We're at home and it's time for bed.

Jacob Houghton (10)
Coniston Primary School, Bristol

Jupiter

I went up to my bedroom,
About to lift the sheet,
When suddenly the floor,
Gave way beneath my feet.

I looked around me, but what to see,
Just black and black, what's this . . . a sack,
I looked within to find a tin,
It shook around, across the ground.

I leapt, I jumped to catch this lump,
I met a stork which started to talk.
I asked for home and in a moan,
It replied, 'Follow the flies.'

I bounded around, without a sound,
I hit a rock, tick-tock, tick-tock.
Huh? It was Jupiter.

David Dunnings (10)
Coniston Primary School, Bristol

Me And My Sister

You and I are always fighting
You get angry and end up biting
One day you say something that's tight
I say, 'OK, you want a fight?'
You said, 'Your mouth is always in operation.'
'Shall we ask Mum for her cooperation?'
As she said that we disappeared
Just as I said sorry, we reappeared . . .
My sister!

Leigh Bevan (10)
Coniston Primary School, Bristol

The Oak Tree

The wise bird flew
And dropped the seed,
The wise bird knew
It was a good deed.

The years went by
And the seed grew,
The birds went high
And the tree was new.

The leaves were green
And the tree tall,
The wind was mean
Leaves started to fall.

The tree was old
Its bark was ripped,
The weather cold
The tree top was clipped.

Daniel Mann (10)
Coniston Primary School, Bristol

O Apple Tree
(Based on 'Song of Hiawatha' by Longfellow)

'Give me your blossom, O apple tree!
Of your beautiful blossom and your fruit,
So to make me a necklace,
That poor people can eat,
That they may taste your fruit'
And the apple tree cheerful and warm,
Laughing through its dark bark,
Giggling like a naughty schoolboy
Answered softly, answered big and round,
'Take my blossom and fruit, O Hiawatha!'
And he took the cheerful reply,
Took the blossom and fruit of the apple tree.

Emily Dowdeswell (10)
Croft Primary School, Painswick

Hiawatha's Canoe

(Based on 'Song of Hiawatha' by Longfellow)

'Give me your nuts O beech tree
Of your golden leaves and your strong branches
So to decorate my canoe with your luscious furry nuts
That people will admire me
That people will appreciate my work'
And the beech tree tall and proud
Wept through its hard and mighty bark
Howled like a werewolf up to the moon
Answered wailing, answered whining
'Take my shiny nuts O Hiawatha'
He took the round nuts
Took the furry leaves
'Thank you O beech tree
Now my canoe will be the best you have ever seen.'

Lydia Thornton (10)
Croft Primary School, Painswick

The Bonsai Tree

(Based on 'Song of Hiawatha' by Longfellow)

'Give me of your flower, O bonsai tree!
Of your petals and your gentle pollen,
So to make my boat more beautiful,
That everyone will stare,
That everyone will see.'
And the bonsai tree small and cute,
Whimpered through its cloak of leaves,
Whimpered like a cowering shrew,
Answered whispering, answered softly,
'Take my flowers O Hiawatha
But be careful and don't waste them, for I have few'
And he took the flowers
Took the gentle pollen of the bonsai tree
And he spread them on the side of the boat
Spread them and made it beautiful.

Kyle Douglass (10)
Croft Primary School, Painswick

The Willow Tree

(Based on 'Song of Hiawatha' by Longfellow)

'Give me your blossom, O willow tree
Of your motherly nature and your kindness
So my boat will be kind
That, the blossom will decorate her
That, the canoe will be caring'
And the beautiful ash tree so lovely and supple
Whimpered through its cloak of bark
Jingle-jangled like a charm bracelet
Answered sobbing, answered blubbering
'Take my branches, O Hiawatha'
And he took the sorrowful branches
Took the pitch-black ash of the ash tree!
To make the rudder for his fine boat
So he could direct his handsome boat.

Cressida Mawdesley-Thomas (10)
Croft Primary School, Painswick

Blossom Tree

(Based on 'Song of Hiawatha' by Longfellow)

'Give me your flowers, O blossom tree
Of your pink flowers and your luscious leaves,
So to decorate my canoe,
That I rush along the river,
That everyone will see me'
And the blossom, bright and colourful,
Shook through its branches,
Shook like a baby's rattle,
Answered wailing, answered weeping,
'Take my flowers, O Hiawatha!'
And he took the pink flowers,
Took the luscious leaves of the blossom tree
And he used the flowers and the leaves
To decorate his canoe.

Evangeline Edgworth (10)
Croft Primary School, Painswick

Cherry Blossom

(Based on 'Song of Hiawatha' by Longfellow)

'Give me of your blossom, O cherry tree!
Of your blossom and your luscious leaves
So to make a pillow so sweet
That I can fall to sleep so fast,
That I may sleep so deeply.'
And the cherry tree, cheerful and round
Shouted happily through its curtain of blossom.
Answered, chanted like a gathering tribe,
Answered fluently, answered flowingly.
'Take my blossom O high Hiawatha!'
And he took the fallen blossom,
Took the luscious leaves off the cherry tree
So Hiawatha took them both.
He wove the leaves and filled the pillow with blossom
O how sweet it smelt upon the evening breeze.

Alicia Barnett (10)
Croft Primary School, Painswick

Yew Tree

(Based on 'Song of Hiawatha' by Longfellow)

'Give me your branches, O yew tree!
Of your twigs and your boughs,
So to make a bow and arrows,
That my land will not starve,
That food be at thy table'
And the yew tree, stubby and strong,
Bellowed through its thick robe of fir,
Bellowing like a lion shuddering the Earth,
Answered strong, answered courageously,
'Take my branches, O Hiawatha!'
And he took the branches of strength,
Took the boughs of the yew tree,
Bending the branches, sharpening the boughs,
To stop his land from starvation.

Felix Gilding (11)
Croft Primary School, Painswick

Blossom Tree

(Based on 'Song of Hiawatha' by Longfellow)

'Give me of your blossom O apple tree
Of your soft white and your pink
So to sit comfortable in my canoe
That I won't hurt myself sitting in wood
That I would be safe from the water
And softness all over my body'
And the cheerful, kind and friendly tree
Through its leaves like an old granny
Answered scared, answered happily
'Take my blossoms O Hiawatha!'
And he took the blossom
Took the blossom of the kind apple tree.

Stephanie Jones (10)
Croft Primary School, Painswick

Red Ant

(Based on 'Tyger, Tyger' by William Blake)

Red ant, red ant crawling slow,
In their nest they eat and glow.
What immortal leg or jaw,
Could crawl across your kitchen floor?

Robert Sidwell (10)
Croft Primary School, Painswick

Horse!

(Based on 'Tyger, Tyger' by William Blake)

Horse! Horse! O galloping fast
In the fields so big and vast
What immortal brain or hand
Could make the beauty of this land?

Abigail Garbett (10)
Croft Primary School, Painswick

The Horse Chestnut Tree

(Based on 'Song of Hiawatha' by Longfellow)

'Give me your chestnuts, O horse chestnut tree
Of your leaves and your bark
So to feed me on my journey
That I may not starve.'
And the horse chestnut tree, wide and tall
Wept through its swaying leaves
Shook like a wet dog
And the horse chestnut tree
Answered weeping, answered sobbing,
'Take my chestnuts Hiawatha.'
So he took the chestnuts and he put them in the canoe
So he would not starve on his journey.

Benjamin Pigott (10)
Croft Primary School, Painswick

Doberman

(Based on 'Tyger, Tyger' by William Blake)

Doberman, Doberman, pouncing to fright
In the darkness of the night
What immortal fang or tail
Would dare bite you and make you wail?

Henry Jackson (10)
Croft Primary School, Painswick

Blue Whale

(Based on 'Tyger, Tyger' by William Blake)

Blue whale, blue whale, you're the king,
In the palace I hear you sing,
What immortal eye or fin,
Could make such a loud din?

Tamara Manton (10)
Croft Primary School, Painswick

The Polar Bear

(Based on 'Tyger, Tyger' by William Blake)

Polar bear, polar bear, white as snow,
In the Arctic, careful and slow,
What immortal eyes or ears,
Could navigate as far as here?

Rebecca Elliott (10)
Croft Primary School, Painswick

Squirrel

(Based on 'Tyger, Tyger' by William Blake)

Squirrel, squirrel, scurry fast
In the trees all tall and vast
What immortal foot or tail
Could scamper so fast round their trail?

Rosemary Davies (11)
Croft Primary School, Painswick

Peregrine Falcon

(Based on 'Tyger, Tyger' by William Blake)

Peregrine, peregrine, swooping low
In the fields of the crow
What immortal eye could see
To catch the prey underneath the tree?

Kyle Douglass (10)
Croft Primary School, Painswick

The Clownfish

(Based on 'Tyger, Tyger' by William Blake)

Clownfish, clownfish, orange and white
In the ocean of the night
What immortal eye or fin
Makes it so bright and thin?

William Jackson (10)
Croft Primary School, Painswick

Rabbit

(Based on 'Tyger, Tyger,' by William Blake)

Rabbit, rabbit, podgy and round,
In the sunshine, on the ground,
What could be so big and fat,
Could be created just like that!

Samuel Andrews (10)
Croft Primary School, Painswick

Chicken

(Based on 'Tyger, Tyger' by William Blake)

Chicken, chicken, small and fat
In the greenest of some flat
What immortal crown or hay
Created a nest so you could lay?

William Moir (10)
Croft Primary School, Painswick

Chelsea Vs Arsenal

They walk through the tunnel,
What's it gonna be?
1-0, 2-0, maybe 3?
The players take the kick-off,
The game is underway,
I wonder what Drogba will do today?

Chelsea have the ball,
Obviously,
Look at this! Lehman is going for a wee!
This is easier than Liverpool,
Because Pires forgot his way to the swimming pool.

Last two minutes,
Still no score,
But the Chelsea attackers look hungry for more,
The Arsenal defenders look worried too,
Henry and Reyes don't know what to do.

Drogba's free kick,
He curls it in!
Chelsea manage to grab the win.

Marley Hall (9)
Farrington Gurney CE Primary School, Bristol

Sound Is All Around Us

Just because we can't see it, doesn't mean it's not there,
Sound is all around us, over here and over there.

My little sister whining, Sammy telling her, 'Shut up!'
The dishwasher whirring as it washes up my cup,
The water in the sink as it starts to fill,
Dorey on the telly saying, 'Look, krill.'

These are some of many sounds that you can hear,
Although you can't see them, now you know they're there.

Lauren Thompson (11)
Farrington Gurney CE Primary School, Bristol

My Eyes

If you would see the world through my eyes
You would see people assisting and caring for each other
Mostly sharing

I see the world differently now
No death, exploding and fighting
No mercy, just pure hate
Racism - where you think you're worth nothing
Just remember

If you look very closely, will you see
All those flowers, parks and beautiful butterflies?
I would
Now this is the right thing to see
Racism is wrong, manners are right

It could be raining outside, but it's warm in my heart.

Hugh Jefferey (9)
Farrington Gurney CE Primary School, Bristol

I Like . . .

I like working, planting bulbs, pulling weeds and picking beans,
I like working, mowing grass, trimming hedges, I'm really keen,
I like working with my dad, washing cars, sweeping up,
I like working with my hands, getting dirty, a real mucky pup,
When my work is finally done, I call my mates and have some fun.

I like being with my friends, playing football, building dens,
I like being with my brother, playing soldiers, making him suffer,
I like riding on my bike, racing up and down is what I like,
I like walking in the rain, jumping in puddles, it drives Mum insane,
I like staying up late at night, watching films that give me a fright,
I like curling up in bed, snuggling up with my *big ted*.

Tom Horman (9)
Farrington Gurney CE Primary School, Bristol

Sk8in

I've been a skater
For as long as I can remember,
I skate to school,
But my dream is to skate an empty pool.

My skateboard is black
With Tony Hawk on the back,
My trucks look plastic
But they're really fantastic.

My wheels are blue
But I really love 'em, I do,
You ought to get a skateboard,
You'll love it too!

I chose my half-pipe,
It arrived on a lorry,
That very same day
I learnt my first ollie.

My favourite trick is a 180°
But I haven't done it lately,
I need my helmet in case I fall
But the chance of that is quite small.

I got a mate who also likes to skate,
He is my dad, oh boy I'm glad!
I ride the ramps that are quite tall,
When I get to the top, people think I'm cool.

One day I want to be on TV
And I want Bart Simpson to come with me!
He's a good skater,
I'm sure I'll see him later.

I started to skate in 1998,
Skateboarding is something I will never hate!

Tom Plummer (10)
Farrington Gurney CE Primary School, Bristol

A Day At The Beach

The sun shone down at the beach.
The waves crashing against the rocks.
The sand tickling my toes.
People eating ice creams along the beach.

Your reflection in the rock pools.
The crabs eating your shadow.
Your shadow has disappeared.
Where has it gone?

The boats bobbing up and down.
The kids playing all around.
The sea hardly makes a sound.
So go and have fun on the beach.

Kirsty Jones (10)
Farrington Gurney CE Primary School, Bristol

The Spider

Spiders come fat, thin, big and small,
They live under the stars and in the hall,
They spin webs to catch their prey,
They do this almost every day.
Tiny flies are today's main course,
The spider is the attacking force,
With lots of babies to feed in its den,
The spider does this again and again.

Jack Gianella (10)
Farrington Gurney CE Primary School, Bristol

Kawasaki

Superbikes racing fast
Speeding round the corners

Superbikes racing fast
Speeding round the track

Superbikes racing fast
Shiny colours gleaming

Superbikes racing fast
Hear the crowd cheer

Superbikes racing fast
See the tyres smoking

Superbikes racing fast
Riding in their leathers

Superbikes racing fast
See them break their records

Superbikes racing fast
Quick, the winner's coming

Superbikes racing fast
Honda, Yamaha, Kawasaki.

Ben Taylor (10)
Farrington Gurney CE Primary School, Bristol

My Puppy, Magic

My puppy, Magic, can be really bad,
She chases her tail as if she were mad.
She bites your trousers and not her toys,
She does this to everyone . . . even the boys.
But when she's asleep,
She doesn't count sheep,
My sister says instead,
She's wetting the bed!

Emma Jones (9)
Farrington Gurney CE Primary School, Bristol

Cats

Cats, cats everywhere,
In boxes,
Under the stairs,
Cats are basically everywhere!
I'm cat crazy,
Can't get enough,
Miaowing for food is
Way too much,
Hissing, scratching,
Purring too,
Happy cats, hungry cats,
Need more food!

Lucy Elliott (9)
Farrington Gurney CE Primary School, Bristol

I Like Ducks

They swim about all day
Quacking at anything that gets in the way
Snap, snap, the sound of their beaks
They don't care just as long as they eat
At night-time they waddle into the shed
And snuggle down quietly on the soft straw bed.

Jordan Malkin (10)
Farrington Gurney CE Primary School, Bristol

Trees

T rees, trees, they sway in the breeze.
R ound and round the wind swirls round them.
E ach tree has a purpose to be there.
E ncyclopaedias can tell you a bit about trees.
S o at the end of the day, the tree is peaceful so they say.

Amy Hillier (9)
Frenchay CE Primary School, Bristol

My Dreams

My dreams would be at Mexico,
For the warm burning sun.
Going to the beaches every day,
For the everlasting fun.

My dreams would be at Australia,
For all the tropical forests.
Seeing mountains, cities and rainbows
And meeting more, new tourists.

My dreams would be at New Zealand,
To go on all the rafts.
Sunbathing in the sun
And making new, different crafts.

My dreams are at south-east Asia,
To see all the fancy dresses.
It would take my breath away,
To visit all these places.

Lucy Quantick (9)
Frenchay CE Primary School, Bristol

My Rabbit, Bubble

My rabbit, Bubble
Likes her cuddles,
She was found under a car,
Cold and wet.
We took her to the vet,
Our clean pet,
She's ended up being loved.

She is happy in her new home,
Lots of places to roam,
She is happy and well,
So everything is swell,
So that's my poem
About our clever little Bubble.

Andrew Smith (9)
Frenchay CE Primary School, Bristol

My Dad

My dad's alright he is,
He isn't afraid of anything,
He can jump right over the moon,
He could wrestle with giants,
My dad can eat like a horse
And swim like a fish.
He's as strong as a gorilla
And as happy as a hippo,
He's as big as a house
And as soft as my teddy.
He's as wise as an owl
And can be crazy too,
He's fantastic at football
And he makes me laugh loads,
I love my dad and he loves me!

Daniel Kembery (9)
Frenchay CE Primary School, Bristol

Seasons

Days are passing,
Years go by,
Winds are blowing in the sky,
Leaves are falling off the trees,
The grass blows in the autumn breeze.

Ella Hayden (9)
Frenchay CE Primary School, Bristol

Honey, The Puppy

H oney, the puppy, was named after honey oh what a pu   P
O nly when she chases the honey bunny for yo   U
N ever, ever the bunny says have a down and up pu   P
E ver or never has the pup have a friend like chocolate the pu   P
Y ou'll always remember that Honey is the best pupp   Y.

Claire Ali (10)
Frenchay CE Primary School, Bristol

Cats And Dogs

C ats stuck in trees
A nd dogs chasing bees
T ogether they're a team
S traying and playing in streams

D oing as they're told
O r misbehaving
G etting very old
S noozing when they're tired.

Laura Brown (10)
Frenchay CE Primary School, Bristol

School

S chool bell rings, the children line up
C harging out for lunch at 12.00
H appy people go out to play
O n goes the school day
O h it's time to go home
L earning is fun but I like it more at home!

Lily Grant (8)
Frenchay CE Primary School, Bristol

Friends

F orever friends, me and my mate.
R unning to school, don't be late.
I see her nearly every day.
E veryone knows we like to play.
N earby all the time.
D eep down inside we are fine.
S pecial friends all of the time.

Georgia Maxwell (9)
Frenchay CE Primary School, Bristol

My Winter Poem

Winter is a
Snowy thing
Sometimes a
Blowy thing
You always
Need a scarf
Gloves and
Hat before
The snow
Goes *splat,*
Splat, splat!

Snowmen are
Fun to build
But not so good
To shield
The eyes and
Nose are made
From carrots
But never made
From parrots

When it rains
We get very wet
Then we need umbrellas
We mustn't forget
So winter is coming
Keep nice and warm
Even in a thunderstorm.

Ella Pullin (7)
Frenchay CE Primary School, Bristol

Autumn

Abandoned leaves
From their trees
Birds are going away
For their holidays
Tanned leaves, red leaves, some still green
Animals hibernating all so keen
Children playing
Trees complaining
Conkers falling
Chestnuts cooking
The sun is hiding
Autumn's coming.

Jemma Kinsey (10)
Frenchay CE Primary School, Bristol

A Summer Evening

Black crows in formation, high up in the sky,
Feathered wings flap frantically, as if they couldn't fly.
Sunset like a fire, the wind rustling in the trees,
Stillness in the air, yet a gentle breeze.

Foxes prowling by the bank, a ripple through a lake,
Hedgehogs nesting in a golden bed, leaves that are still to fall and flake.
The smell of gold ripe corn, the last ray of summer sun,
Fawns galloping, kicking up clouds of dust and decay as they run.

Calm, rolling hills of emerald and rubies,
Jade and sapphires, bluebells and poppies,
Soothing and cooling as love,
The sun on the sea, as light on a dove.

All these things I love so well.
Nightingales chirping, roses pure white,
The frolicking lambs like snow-covered swans,
The elegant dove to the solitary night.

Ella Williams (8)
Kempsford CE (VC) Primary School, Kempsford

Hallowe'en

On Hallowe'en when church bells chime,
Twelve at midnight is the time,
Witches, skeletons, gravediggers too,
Will come to your doorstep and haunt you.
Look outside and smell the air,
Of witch's brew from her spooky lair,
It's packed with potions, toe of bat,
It can even turn you into a venomous cat.
Warlocks zooming around on broomsticks,
Doing dangerous and thrilling tricks,
So remember when it is Hallowe'en,
Don't go to sleep because it's time to scream . . .
Aaaargh!

David Mather (9)
Kempsford CE (VC) Primary School, Kempsford

Space Tour

The cold, terrifying darkness surrounds us
We approach some dazzling stars
The moon swaying calmly in the darkness
The spaceman floating in the breeze
Finally, the light floats up into the air.

Daragh Smith (9)
Kempsford CE (VC) Primary School, Kempsford

Animals

I spoke of barking dogs sprinting like an athlete.
I spoke of splashing dolphins leaping like a gymnast.
I spoke of cute koala bears crawling like a baby.
I spoke of charging elephants squirting like a crystal fountain.
I spoke of fluffy rabbits jumping like a spring.
I spoke, I spoke, I spoke.

Emily Hepworth (9)
Kempsford CE (VC) Primary School, Kempsford

Hope

Hope is all I need to get through a roaring, bashing storm
Hope is like a quiet, blooming flower
Hope is a lion sleeping through the hot, sunny afternoon
Hope is like a praising priest baptising a baby
Hope is an angel floating down to Earth to take me home to Heaven
Hope is all I need to get through the world.

CanJarri McKinley (8)
Kempsford CE (VC) Primary School, Kempsford

Jet Plane, Jet Plane

Jet plane, jet plane in the sky,
Roaring engines flying by,
Taking passengers from A to B,
From New York to Sydney,
Looking high into the sky above,
Leaving vapour trails - the kiss of love,
My best friend, Cameron, will soon fly off to Bahrain,
I just hope we meet again.

Callum Cornish (8)
Kempsford CE (VC) Primary School, Kempsford

My Cat

My cat, Itchy, reminds me of a warm, cosy, black sofa.
He is ginger, golden like a special coin.
Itchy is a fresh, tasty melon that looks really small.
He is a soft, gentle summer breeze.
Itchy is a licking cat with a tongue as rough as sandpaper.

Connor Denness (8)
Kempsford CE (VC) Primary School, Kempsford

Slowly

Slowly the tiger stalks its prey,
Slowly the clouds cross the day.
Slowly the mole tunnels under the ground,
Slowly the ancient bones are found.

Slowly the Earth turns around,
Slowly the ants build their mound.
Slowly the trees grow so high,
Slowly the baby begins to cry.

Slowly the whale swims through the sea,
Slowly the pupa turns into a bee.
Slowly the fire turns to ash,
Slowly the grass gives you a rash.

Slowly the planets orbit the sun,
Slowly the baker bakes a bun.
Slow is the snail - but slowest of all
Is the ivy spreading along the old brick wall.

Thomas Windsor (8)
Kempsford CE (VC) Primary School, Kempsford

The Postman

One letter for the 'Whites',
A postcard for the 'Kats',
Two parcels for the . . . hang on,
They don't live here anymore, the 'Bats'.

Some boots sent to Jon Seed,
Who lives down the road,
That's very cool indeed!

Ellie Wrona (9)
Kempsford CE (VC) Primary School, Kempsford

All About Me

True Britt is my name,
Happy as ever is my fame,
Capricorn am I, you see,
My family live in Kempsford with me.

Leopards are to be my best,
Better animals than the rest.
Emily and Holly are my best friends,
That is how the story ends.

But suddenly I've thought of more,
Of learning history galore.
Blue are my eyes, brown is my hair,
Born in Swindon, move here and there.

That is all about me!

Kristy Britt (9)
Kempsford CE (VC) Primary School, Kempsford

A Day At The Seaside

Dolphins diving through the waves,
Children hiding in the caves,
Families playing in the sand,
Some with ice creams in their hand!

People jumping off the pier,
Some without any fear,
Fluffy clouds floating by,
In the bright shining sky.

How nice it is to be,
To sit beside the sea,
But guess what . . .
I can't wait till next summer!

Emily Guthrie (9)
Kempsford CE (VC) Primary School, Kempsford

My Puppy

Sooty plays footy while he's looking very pretty
He's very lovely when he's just been washed with bubbly
He's called Sooty because he's black like soot
We have lots of fun when he chases my foot
We take long walks in the woods and when he chases bunnies
He looks kind of funny
He races off with his ears flapping up and down
When I call him back he looks like a circus clown
All covered in leaves, mud and sticks
He plays lots of games with our dog, Scruffy
Who is brown and fluffy.

Lacey Moulden (9)
Kempsford CE (VC) Primary School, Kempsford

The River's Life

Running swiftly through the dale,
Seems so steep compared to the gale.
Through the rocky mountains lies
Has the reflection of the skies.
Leads into the estuaries, out to the sea,
It's a symbol of freedom, to be free
And suddenly the current grew tight,
But the river went on, right into the night!

Emily Dixon-Fallon (10)
Kempsford CE (VC) Primary School, Kempsford

Pitch-Black

Pitch-black, as dark as black ink
Rocks fragmented all over space with tiny specks of diamonds in
Stars glittering in the shadow of the Earth
The moon shimmering as the night gets darker and darker
Mysterious aliens bouncing on the planet Mars.

Sarah White (10)
Kempsford CE (VC) Primary School, Kempsford

Help

Help, help
Thine young is scattered
Torrential storm blowing
Help, help

Help, help
Thy hiding place gone
Food supply deserted
Help, help

Help, help
There's hunters loose
The lake is flooded
Help, help

Help, help
Thine young is scattered
Torrential storm blowing
Help, help

Help, help
They're not returned
Bang! Bang!
They're gone
Help, help.

George Irving (10)
Kempsford CE (VC) Primary School, Kempsford

My Secret Unicorn

My secret unicorn is as secret as secrets can be,
My secret unicorn loves me.

She dances and prances with the butterflies,
I can see the twinkle that shines in her eyes.

She's stronger than magic and always knows her way,
I love her very much so I've called her May.

Annabel Stagg (8)
Kempsford CE (VC) Primary School, Kempsford

The Tickle Rhyme

'Who's that tickling my back?' said the wall.
'Me,' said a caterpillar learning to crawl.

'Who's that tickling my leg?' said the house.
'Me,' said a small ladybird, 'I'm learning to fly.'

'Who's that tickling my face?' said a tree.
'Me,' said a small, hairy worm learning how to slide.

'Who's that tickling my head?' said a cat.
'Me,' said a fly, 'I'm learning to fly.'

'Who's that tickling my arm?' said a cow.
'Me,' said a greenfly, 'I'm learning how to slide.'

'Who's that tickling my eye?' said a goat.
'Me,' said a small caterpillar, 'I'm learning how to fly now!'

Ellie Maundrell (7)
Kempsford CE (VC) Primary School, Kempsford

The Stormy Night

(Based on 'Tyger, Tyger' by William Blake)

Tiger, tiger burning bright,
In the middle of the night,
Tiger, tiger so, so scared,
Tiger, tiger never cared.

Tiger, tiger wants to get out,
Tiger, tiger wants to shout!
Tiger, tiger terrified,
Tiger, tiger wants to hide!

Tiger, tiger ever so fierce,
Tiger, tiger his claws do pierce.

Tiger, tiger burning bright,
In the middle of the night,
Tiger, tiger so, so scared,
Tiger, tiger never cared.

Sophie Cornish (11)
Kempsford CE (VC) Primary School, Kempsford

The White Dragon

The white dragon is a shy lizard,
Who lives high in the mountains
And doesn't even care of a blizzard,
His flame is as white as crystal snow
And could freeze you in one blow,
His scales are as smooth as skin
And has a fluffy beard under his chin,
His home is a dark, dark cave
And to enter the cost is to be brave,
The dragon is one short of a friend,
That is all I'm afraid,
It has come . . .
To an end.

Joseph Housley (9)
Kempsford CE (VC) Primary School, Kempsford

Flowers!

F lowers are pretty
L ovely and bright
O uch, some are prickly
W ow, some are nice
E verywhere there are flowers
R ed ones, yellow, blue and green
S pecial in every way.

Nicola Axel-Berg (7)
Kempsford CE (VC) Primary School, Kempsford

All Out At Night

The rainbow-coloured planets dazzling in the night.
The massive spaceship floating in space.
The murky, black, freezing cold night.
The whizzing rockets shooting above you.

Lucy Gray (9)
Kempsford CE (VC) Primary School, Kempsford

Ponies In The Countryside

Ponies canter, ponies gallop
Through open fields and countryside.

Ponies roll, ponies jump
Over high fences and ditches.

Ponies feel soft,
Thick coats, flicking tails
Twitching ears, grunting noses.

I love listening to ponies' hooves
Shattering the pavements.

Beth Hallam (9)
Kempsford CE (VC) Primary School, Kempsford

Confusion

Confusion is a multicoloured never-ending spiral,
Confusion is too confusing to smell,
Confusing tastes like pasta with no taste,
Confusion is too high-pitched to be heard,
It feels soft but hard,
Confusion lives in a brain with no idea,
Confusion is an unfinished puzzle.

David Caswell (10)
Kempsford CE (VC) Primary School, Kempsford

Chocolate

Once upon a rhyme there was a thing called chocolate
Everyone loved it and ate it all the time
Until one terrible day (well, it wasn't so bad for me)
I ate all the chocolate
Now all the kids were unhappy and begged me to give it back
So I did . . .

Holly Strange (9)
Kempsford CE (VC) Primary School, Kempsford

Autumn

The leaves are falling to
           the ground because
   autumn's coming.
              Shhh! listen to the
rustling leaves.
      The wind is
blowing and
          the rain is falling.
I'm glad that
     autumn has come
   but now it has gone.

Alice Green (7)
Kempsford CE (VC) Primary School, Kempsford

Harvest Festival

Peaches, grapes and pears,
For everyone who cares,
Tasty rice, oats and corn,
Like food with natural goodness.

We will share our food,
To all the people in our world,
As we go to a harvest festival,
We celebrate this special gift!

Amy Russell (10)
Kempsford CE (VC) Primary School, Kempsford

Guilt

Guilt is a dark growing patch inside the soul
Guilt tastes like polluted air
Guilt sounds like an alarm bell going off through your head
It feels like the Devil is taking over your body
Guilt lives in the heart of the Devil.

Thomas Hallam (10)
Kempsford CE (VC) Primary School, Kempsford

Spacemen Exploring

Dark, spooky night, pitch-black sky.
Stars twinkling in the yellow sparkling sky.
Spacemen sprinting around the moon fighting aliens.
Rockets zooming around and exploring.
Aliens searching for food, being funny and scary.

Joseph James (9)
Kempsford CE (VC) Primary School, Kempsford

My War

I would fight for peace,
I would attack all danger,
I would battle for love and hope
    And surrender to happiness.

I would battle for love,
I would fight against all evil,
I would attack guns and bombs
    And surrender to hope.

Jordan Bryan (10)
Norton Primary School, Gloucester

My War

I would blitz terrorism with peace,
I would destroy hate with truth,
I would kill dictatorship with freedom
And surrender to love and hope.

I would battle for love,
I would fight for peace,
I would drive away all those evil things
And surrender to all that is good.

Rhys Baird (10)
Norton Primary School, Gloucester

If I Ruled The World (My War)

I would battle through coughing clouds,
Crusade with songs of hope,
I would attack terrors of war,
I would surrender to the truth.

Amy Spiers (9)
Norton Primary School, Gloucester

War Is . . .

War is a silent shark leading you into its trap,
War is a pit of snakes waiting for their prey,
War is a tiger shark stalking under the ocean,
War is a lake filled with crocodiles waiting for their prey.

Sam Steel (9)
Norton Primary School, Gloucester

War Smells!

War is a gas smell in the air waiting to suffocate us!
War is a smell of damp and soggy air with blood on the floor.
War is a salty water smell of people crying and boats sinking.
War is not a fresh air smell because of bombs and chemical gases.

Marykate Bowers (10)
Norton Primary School, Gloucester

War Animals

War is a lion fighting over territory.
War is a snake rattling its warning.
War is an eagle starring at his prey.
War is a snake spraying poison all around.
War is a scabby leopard chasing his prey.

Rosie Evans (9)
Norton Primary School, Gloucester

When Will It End, Mummy?

When will it end, Mummy?
I don't like the sound,
It scares me very much
When it hits the ground.

When will it end, Mummy?
There's big explosions going mad,
Very little light,
When will Daddy be home with stories at night?

Chantelle Packman (9)
Norton Primary School, Gloucester

My War

I would fight for happiness,
I would kill the war.
I would destroy danger
And surrender to hope.

I would invade anger,
I would battle for peace.
I would attack loneliness
And surrender to love.

Lucy Jones (10)
Norton Primary School, Gloucester

If I Ruled The World

If I ruled the world
I'd kill loneliness with hope
I would attack danger with love
I would ambush hate with courage
I would surrender to love.

Laurence Anscombe (9)
Norton Primary School, Gloucester

My War

I would attack lies with truth,
I would attack hate with courage,
I would attack anger with hope
And surrender to love.

I would assault anger,
I would ambush lies,
I would invade hate
And surrender to peace.

I would fight for freedom,
I would battle for peace,
I would conquer loneliness
And surrender to hope.

Jack Steel (11)
Norton Primary School, Gloucester

If I Ruled The World

I will bombard loneliness with friends,
I will fight for freedom with courage,
I will attack fear with hope strongly,
I will destroy chaos with my heart.

I will stop terrorism with help,
I will dispose of war for good,
I will vanish drugs from the world,
I will make the world a place of happiness.

Ryan Merry (10)
Norton Primary School, Gloucester

My War

I would battle for peace,
I would fight for love,
I would invade loneliness
And surrender to hope.

I would battle for happiness,
I would fight for freedom,
I would combat danger
And surrender to love.

I would battle for hope,
I would fight for pride,
I would attack war
And surrender to peace.

Mark Kerry (10)
Norton Primary School, Gloucester

My War

I would battle for happiness,
I would fight for freedom,
I would attack lies
And surrender to peace.

I would invade danger,
I would battle for hope,
I would destroy attacks,
I would surrender to love.

Emily Stagg (10)
Norton Primary School, Gloucester

What War Smells Like

The war has a strong smell of different things,
It smells of dusty rubble falling down,
Of smoke and buildings burning,
It smells of wet, squidgy mud.

The air is filled with poisoned gas,
Gunpowder and tank fumes too.
The sky is filled with the smell of fresh rainwater,
Mixed with the smell of dust and ashes.

It smells of burning wood,
It's a smell of guns and bombs falling to the ground.
It smells of petrol leaking from tanks and planes
And that is what war smells like.

Charlotte Smith (10)
Norton Primary School, Gloucester

The Second World War

They tried to kill their enemy,
Lots of people died,
It was a very sad time
For people left behind.

The English killed Hitler,
The English won victorious,
The Germans lost, defeated
And the English are English again.

Erica Webb (10)
Norton Primary School, Gloucester

Evacuated

New life starts,
Don't know where, don't know when,
New family starts,
Don't know where, don't know when,
New school starts,
Don't know where, don't know when,
New friends starts,
Don't know where, don't know when,
New war will start,
Don't know where, don't know when,
Don't know why.

Carys Owen (9)
Norton Primary School, Gloucester

By The Sea

I love playing
Beside the sea,
It's lots of fun
For Matthew and me.

We build sandcastles
And look for shells,
We eat ice creams
Until our tummies swell.

We look in rock pools
And find starfish and crabs,
We'll take them home
And hide them under the slabs.

The tide comes in
The sand disappears,
Better go quickly or
We'll sink up to our ears!

Siân Whitehorn (8)
Portishead Primary School, Portishead

My Apple Tree

I have an apple tree in my garden,
I pick the apples for my mum,
She makes apple pies for my tum,
I climb my apple tree very high,
So I can touch the sky,
I have a swing on my tree,
My dad put it there for me,
I love my apple tree.

Thomas Clark (8)
Portishead Primary School, Portishead

The Sea

I live by the sea,
It's a nice place to be,
I would like to have a boat
With a big yellow coat,
I would watch the fish
And I could make a wish,
My friends would be with me
And play with me by the sea.

Charlotte Clements (7)
Portishead Primary School, Portishead

Fire

Fire is sparkly, yellow, orange and red,
It's hot and flamey,
Glowing in the chilly night,
It spread its fierce flames,
Fire keeps you warm when you are cold.

Ella Whittle (8)
Portishead Primary School, Portishead

My Dog, Moby

I have a dog called Moby
We haven't had him long
He's brown and tan in colour
And very, very strong!

We have had him from a puppy
He didn't want to come
He cried and cried the first night
Because he missed his mum

But now he's very happy
At his new home
He has a bed and a blanket
And loves chewing on his bone

His breed is a Doberman
Which makes some people scared
He loves all his family
But burglars better beware

I love my dog called Moby
He's a very good friend to me
He makes me smile when I'm sad
And that's good enough for me.

Jess Burns (8)
Portishead Primary School, Portishead

Birds

You get pretty ones.
You get dull ones.
Some are so colourful.
Some are very rare.
Some live in the water.
Some live in nests.
You get different types of birds.

Poppy Manning (8)
Portishead Primary School, Portishead

At Night

At night it's dark outside,
There are strange noises,
Animals scuttling around,
People talking and laughing,
The night's a wonderful time.

The night's sometimes still,
Just a gentle breeze,
Maybe one or two cars,
Nothing else you would hear,
The night's a silent time.

The night's sometimes noisy,
People screaming, people arguing,
Dogs barking, cats miaowing,
Trees banging on the window,
The night's a noisy time.

The night's sometimes scary,
People moving when everyone's asleep,
Creaking noises and taps dripping,
Cars suddenly beeping,
The night's a scary time.

The night's sometimes stormy,
The rain spitting and splashing on the rooftops,
Rough, stormy wind fills the air,
It is very cold in this type of weather,
The night's a stormy time,
The night's a great time!

Freya Park (8)
Portishead Primary School, Portishead

My Grandpa

My grandpa is a great person to have around.
He is artistic, funny, scientific and kind.
My grandpa is the same person as me really
And he is the *best* grandpa in the world.

My grandpa is a great person to have around.
He is creative, imaginative and determined.
My grandpa has a little white shed
And he is the *best* grandpa in the world.

My grandpa is a great person to have around.
He is mischievous, a great cook and adventurous.
My grandpa makes me feel excited
And he is the *best* grandpa in the world.

My grandpa is a great person to have around.
He is good at chess and at helping with projects.
My grandpa makes me feel happy
And he is the *best* grandpa in the world.

Olivia Pointon (8)
Portishead Primary School, Portishead

Night

The sun has fallen,
Night has arrived,
The birds have sung one last time.

The street lamps are glowing,
But darkness still rules,
The birds have sung one last time.

The owls are swooping down through the trees,
Rats scurrying everywhere!
The birds have sung one last time.

The sun has come out again,
Hip hip hooray! The sun's come out . . .
And the birds are singing again!

Joel Hopkins (8)
Portishead Primary School, Portishead

School

School is fun
School is great
School is where we learn
School is where we learn to read and write
But we don't go there at night
School is where we learn to add and take away
As we move up years work gets even harder
School is where we learn to add money
School is where we learn about history
School is where we learn to write poems
School is where we learn to write stories.

Thomas Kimberley (8)
Portishead Primary School, Portishead

My Friends

I don't know how many friends I've got,
But it seems to be quite a lot.
They all are different, every one,
But together we all have lots of fun.

Friends are funny, friends can play,
Friends are fantastic any day.
I see my friends each day at school,
We chat and laugh, my friends are *cool!*

Emily Wall (8)
Portishead Primary School, Portishead

There Was A Young Boy

There was a young boy from Portishead
Who couldn't get out of his bed
He slept all day
In his bed he lay
And only got out to be fed!

William Instance (8)
Portishead Primary School, Portishead

From My Window

Leaves falling from the autumn trees
At noon
Winding and twisting
Like a dancer
It's beautiful
Ever-changing colours on the ground
At noon
Sparkling and shimmering
Like a glittering coat
It's beautiful
Muddy footprints in the fields
At noon
Dark and sloppy
Like a dark winter's day
It's disastrous!

Ellie Smith (9)
Raysfield Junior School, Chipping Sodbury

From My Window

Leaves of the autumn tree
At sunrise
Falling and tumbling
Like precipitation
It's amazing
Conkers rolling down the hill
At sunrise
Spinning and rotating
Like wheels on a skateboard
It's amazing
A conker wrapped up in its shell
At daybreak
Green and spiky
Like a bird in its egg, fantastic.

Adam Turton (9)
Raysfield Junior School, Chipping Sodbury

The River

The river is a tiger,
Leaping off cliffs,
Plunging down waterfalls.

The river is a cobra,
Slithering down the mountain,
Slipping down the hill.

The river is a shadow,
Lurking in the deep,
With an unknown origin.

But the river is a soother,
A healer in disguise,
All of these the river is,
As it stares at you with blue eyes.

Cameron Hector (9)
Raysfield Junior School, Chipping Sodbury

What Is The River?

The river is a kitty cat,
It cusses and pounces,
Right over rocks, it rolls around,
As quick as a flash.

The river is a slithering snake,
It swishes and swirls,
It slithers and hisses,
As loud as it can.

The river is a wriggly worm,
It wiggles in and out making his way around,
It rolls over rocks
As easy as that.

The river is a black bull,
It tears down trees, smashes into rocks,
It invades whole streets
Before you can say his name, bull.

Katie Hooper (9)
Raysfield Junior School, Chipping Sodbury

What Is The River?

The river is a daydreamer
It shimmers and glides
Through the slow-flowing river

The river's a wriggler
Like it's got ants in its pants
Through the countryside
Making it look like a knight in shining armour

The river's a snake
Like a fierce cobra
Slithering down the river

The river's a taxi
Picking up bits of rock
And rubbish and
Sometimes it will take your car!

The river's a fast flower
Splashing through rocks.

Alex McMillan (9)
Raysfield Junior School, Chipping Sodbury

What Is The River?

The river is a sparkle,
That gleams up to the sun.

The river is a cobra,
Who slithers through the grass.

The river is a knight's shining armour,
Who will charge at you all day.

The river is a diamond ring,
Who will flash with beauty.

The river is all those things,
But watch out, you'll never know where he will strike again!

Mitchell Evans (9)
Raysfield Junior School, Chipping Sodbury

What Is The River?

The river is a fisher right down below,
Swallowing fish, watch as you go.
The river is a knight in shining armour,
Glinting and glimmering, shining in the sun.
The river is a copy-cat, reflecting the moon,
Trapped and about to be swallowed!
The river is a wriggly worm, meandering and twisting,
Does it even know the way?
The river is a pop star getting more popular every day,
Dancing to his beat.
The river is a pair of scissors,
Snipping and cutting its way to the sea.
The river is a fighter,
Pushing and shoving all the rocks.
The river is a wanderer, going really slow,
He meanders and curves.
The river is a true friend, joining together to be mighty.

Natasha Kilbane (9)
Raysfield Junior School, Chipping Sodbury

The River

The river is a hotel,
Where the fish come to stay,
In and out of rivers,
To have a nice holiday!
The river is a ghost,
Flying past the banks,
It's a nasty poltergeist
And loves to play lots of pranks!
The river is a tube,
Rushing by the station,
Only slowing down to stop
And pick up the lovely fish of the nation!
The river is a taxi,
Picking up the fish.
If you want a ride,
It will pick you up like a ride.
The river is a robber,
Picking up things you drop,
He won't give them back
Or else he would have stopped!

Rebecca Biggs (9)
Raysfield Junior School, Chipping Sodbury

The River

The river is a thin shoelace,
Long and milky-white,
Jumping over rocks,
Flapping in the wispy winds.

The river is a daydreamer,
Calmly swooping by,
Sparkling as it whooshes on,
Shimmers like the night sky . . .

The river is a snake,
Hissing as it slithers,
Weaving in and out the rocks,
Splashing as it goes on and on.

The river is a ballerina,
Prancing in its glamorous tutu,
Pushing back its sleek hair,
Twirling as it dances on.

Harriet Dean (9)
Raysfield Junior School, Chipping Sodbury

What Is The River?

The river is a footballer
That kicks the pebbles away
And the pebble is in the goal

The river is a yellow taxi
That picks up all the stones
And drops them off at the waterfall

The river is a bulldozer
That strikes through the rocks
Don't stand in its way or you will be next!

The river is a snake
That curves and meanders
And pounds all the stones out of the way

The river is a fighter
That smashes all the rocks -
Do not fall over!

Ben Weaver (9)
Raysfield Junior School, Chipping Sodbury

My Favourite Things

My teddy is so cool
He makes me feel I rule the school!
He is pink
He makes me think!
He wears a bow
Can I show?
He is soft
Too good to go in the loft!
His eyes are blue
Just like you!

Katie Davies (8)
Tibberton Community Primary School, Tibberton

The Rugby Fiasco

Every player on the pitch figures it out
Except for me
I'm the faint one
A Gloucester rugby player . . . I really ain't one

People say I really stand out
So does the coach
But I really doubt

So I will pack my bags
And leave this little game
I am so inexperienced
I can't even remember the coach's name

I'm just about to reach the gate
When this little voice said
'Hello mate'

What I heard
I had heard never
From then on
We carried this game on together.

Tom Heathfield (8)
Tibberton Community Primary School, Tibberton

Dragons! Dragons!

D ragon! Dragon! on the wall
R aging wings so tall, so tall
A nger, anger so loud
G rubby, grubby, so fast and cruel
O verwhelmed. We are overwhelmed
N ervous people running so fast.
S uddenly I wake up. Morning has come!

Oliver Beale (9)
Tibberton Community Primary School, Tibberton

Who Am I?

I arch my neck,
Ears prick up,
Nostrils flare.

My flowing mane dances and shimmers
In the glittering sun,
My tail is enough to overwhelm a king.

My hooves thunder along the dusty path,
Shining and twinkling in the murky landscape,
I stop and my front legs leave the ground
As I break into a tremendous rear.

Watch me,
See me
Paw the air,
Who am I
Pawing the air?

I'm a horse,
A splendid Arab am I,
That's what I am,
An elegant stallion is me.

Wednesday Batchelor (10)
Tibberton Community Primary School, Tibberton

My Prize

My prize is as lovely as the glittering, sparkling moon.
When I wear my prize I feel like the Queen.
I would be honoured to wear my prize.
My precious prize is who I am!
Who I am is my precious prize!
Yes!
It is my necklace!

Catherine Goodwin (9)
Tibberton Community Primary School, Tibberton

I Want To Be A Tooth Fairy

I want to be a tooth fairy
Flying in the bright blue sky
I will carry white shiny teeth
I will cheer up the young
By giving them a pound!
I really want to be a tooth fairy
Flying in the bright blue sky!

Abigail Pearce (7)
Tibberton Community Primary School, Tibberton

Autumn

A sleeping hedgehog,
its last few moments
before its darkest sleep.
A golden carpet covering the world.
Everything is fading . . . fading away.

Callum Hall (10)
Tibberton Community Primary School, Tibberton

My Favourite Things

A hot bubbly bath with my rubber duck
Floating on the foamy water
A cosy, warm and springy bed
Resting my head on my squidgy, woolly pillow
A nice nap
A jam sandwich with crispy, crunchy crisps!

Declan Beale (7)
Tibberton Community Primary School, Tibberton

Chris

He's an inflatable cupboard that opens and closes in on you.
He's a gorilla capable of knocking a tree down in one punch!
He's Hell if you're annoying,
He's Heaven if you're not.
He's a screaming sausage baking gently in the oven.
He's a red sunrise after a silent, starless night.
My brother, Chris.

David Burns (9)
Warden Hill Primary School, Cheltenham

Alexander

He is a pillow, who always keeps me awake when I go to sleep,
He is a snappy crocodile, who hates having jokes played on him,
He is a busy New York street,
He is a ringing alarm clock that never stops
And a bright sparkling sunny morning that makes you smile,
My friend, *Alex.*

Oliver Blay (9)
Warden Hill Primary School, Cheltenham

My Uncle John

He is a comfortable, relaxing sofa.
He is a clever, cunning fox always figuring things out.
He is a slow drifting lilo grabbing you across the shore.
A whisper spoken but sometimes spoken loud.
An early sunset ready to end the adventure.

Jake Heath (10)
Warden Hill Primary School, Cheltenham

My Cousin

She is a bouncy mattress always on the move,
She is a bouncy kangaroo jumping time and time again
She is a bustling town always moving
She is a whistling bird on a hot, sunny day
She is a hot, hurrying person that runs around day and night
That's my cousin, *Jade.*

Lauren Lewis (9)
Warden Hill Primary School, Cheltenham

My Friend, Matt

A wooden plank to be sawn but not to be hurt.
A cheetah drooling as he is catching his prey.
A big city in Cyprus.
A huge tan and very sunny.
A calm voice same as his brother's and sister.
He's 12 o'clock waiting to play football.
My friend, *Matthew.*

Jack Kelly (10)
Warden Hill Primary School, Cheltenham

My Cuddly Mum

She is a big beanbag soft and cuddly.
She is a yapping dog when I don't tidy my room.
She is like a front room knitting a cardigan.
She is like a loud person splashing in a puddle
And a silent night sleeping happily.
My cuddly mum.

Hannah Martin (9)
Warden Hill Primary School, Cheltenham

My Friend

He is a TV when he is happy,
A charging bull that's fierce and strong when he is playing
foot: football or racing,
A swimming pool that's deep,
A lorry horn in the playground that is very loud,
He is a bright and sunny day when he is having a good time,
My friend, Jack.

Adam Dunlop (9)
Warden Hill Primary School, Cheltenham

My Friend

He is a funny joker, who makes you laugh your head off.
He is a sprinting cheetah after his prey.
He is a wooden chair to be there if you are hurt
And a referee's whistle, shrill and quick.
An afternoon visiting friends, making a den, playing football.
My friend, Harvey!

James Kear (9)
Warden Hill Primary School, Cheltenham

My Brother, Dominic

He is a solid mattress jumping on you,
He is a kind father lion looking after his cubs,
He is the grass on a windy day blowing in the breeze,
He is like the sun going down,
He is a grunting pig when he is asleep.

Jamie Todd (9)
Warden Hill Primary School, Cheltenham

My Lovely Mum

She is as busy as a spider in the morning making breakfast
for all my family,
She is a soft and cuddly cushion always comforting me,
She is a warm tropical beach with a light breeze,
A fluffy kitten caring and sleeping on the sofa,
She is a soft lullaby singing me to sleep,
My lovely mum!

Holly Isherwood (9)
Warden Hill Primary School, Cheltenham

My Grandpa

He is a bouncy chair who makes you laugh
He is like a hilarious monkey swinging from branch to branch
He is a circus full of laughing people
A car horn hooting, getting attention
He's a sunny morning walking quickly
With eager dogs barking loudly
My grandpa.

Jonathan Rosagro (9)
Warden Hill Primary School, Cheltenham

My Friend, Jack

Jack is a bouncy chair springy and fun.
He is a galloping stag running through the forest.
He is an Olympic sprinter in Athens.
He is a football crowd, *'United! United!'*
He is like the sun rising on a bright morning.
My friend, Jack.

Harvey Phelps (10)
Warden Hill Primary School, Cheltenham

My Friend, Matti

He is a comfortable bed with strong, hard legs,
A silver fish in the sea swimming a long distance,
He is a football pitch playing for United,
A cheepy-chirpy boy running a long distance,
A jolly morning that has a tongue that cheers me up
whenever I am sad.
My great mate, Matti.

Ben Harris (10)
Warden Hill Primary School, Cheltenham

My Brother

My brother, Rob, is a cheeky monkey and is quite funky.
He is a funny, red-nosed clown who cheers me up when I am down.
He's as loud as an elephant running up and down a hotel corridor.
He is a clever calculator, but not a very good skater!
In the morning he's a lazy hippo stomping down the stairs.
That's my brother!

Elena Ferro Kirby (9)
Warden Hill Primary School, Cheltenham

My Brother, Sami

He is a hard chair that wobbles about,
He is a big eagle that flies in the bright blue sky,
He is a miserable park that nobody visits,
He's a whistle when he runs around in the playground,
He is a bright star when he is happy,
My brother, Sami.

Ahbab Rahman (9)
Warden Hill Primary School, Cheltenham

My Cousin

She is a soft silk cushion always kind and thoughtful,
A speedy greyhound when she is running round the track,
She is a fun park always taking me out and making me laugh,
She is a humongous drum, chatting away,
A tasty lunchtime always treating me to fancy cakes and pastries,
My cousin, Tammana.

Selina Islam (10)
Warden Hill Primary School, Cheltenham

My Mum

She is a clever computer always thinking.
She is an owl swooping down for a mouse or two.
She is soft as cotton wool, rubbing against your cheek.
Her voice is soft when she gently sleeps.
She is an evening cuddling up by the fire drinking hot chocolate.

Ellie Pitt (9)
Warden Hill Primary School, Cheltenham

My Brother

My brother is a rock-solid table, reliable, dependable,
He is a little tiger cub drifting off to sleep,
He's a splashing swimming pool drenching you,
He's a screaming crowd,
He's a sunset gently closing his eyes,
He is my little brother, Joshua.

Ryan Wiggett-Parker (10)
Warden Hill Primary School, Cheltenham

Two Girls I Know

They're both bouncy chairs all kind and cheerful,
Both excited hyenas laughing all day long,
They're both a lift moving slowly up and down,
Two trumpets playing in a band, *toot! toot!*
The sunrise waking up your bright morning.
I suppose it is true that there are some things the same
Two girls I know!

Heather Didcote (9)
Warden Hill Primary School, Cheltenham

My Second Cousin, Robin

He's a hard, wooden chair with a soft blue cushion,
He is a big grizzly bear who's a big softy,
He's a gym with lots of weights and rowing machines,
He is a loud disco with old-fashioned music,
My second cousin, Robin!

Elayna Cambridge (9)
Warden Hill Primary School, Cheltenham

My Sister

She is a screaming teddy bear that loves me,
A proud peacock peering in the mirror,
A fairy-filled room admiring and vain,
An angry fist thudding into my stomach,
A Saturday morning screaming in my ear,
My sister!

Kaye Pollard (9)
Warden Hill Primary School, Cheltenham

My Mum

She is a soft cuddly cushion that wraps me in warmth,
She is an excited rabbit always springing about,
A rumbling roller coaster ride, fun but screaming,
She is a hummingbird and likes to smell flowers,
A fine sunny morning that plays with you,
My mum!

Holly Smith (9)
Warden Hill Primary School, Cheltenham

My Cat, Minstrel

As soft as a sofa, out of control.
She is a cuddly, soft tiger purring wildly.
A comfy bedroom with a cosy bed.
A loud, howling cat calling for help.
She is a cheetah in the bright moonlight.
Prowling mouse quiet.
Shh, it's top secret!

Samantha Rawlings (10)
Warden Hill Primary School, Cheltenham

My Cousin, Holly

A springy mattress when she's happy,
A kangaroo bouncing around over and over and over again,
She's the crashing waves, twisting and tumbling,
A music station always playing noisy music,
She's an early morning, bright and cheery,
My cousin, Holly.

Sam Wedley (9)
Warden Hill Primary School, Cheltenham

My Friend, Ben

He's a funny joker who makes you laugh so you can't stop,
He is a speedy cheetah when he starts to sprint,
He's a wooden chair who stands up for you when you get hurt,
He's the cheering of a crowd when he's joyful,
A stormy night when he's angry,
My friend, Ben.

Matt Street (9)
Warden Hill Primary School, Cheltenham

My Best Friend

She is a soft, cuddly, fluffy pillow, always warm and happy.
She is a bouncy, friendly rabbit always jumping and skipping.
She's like Cadbury World, thick, chocolatey and sweet.
She is a CD player always thundering and loud.
She is a bright, big sunflower always prettier than the rest.
My best friend!

Romillie Compton (9)
Warden Hill Primary School, Cheltenham

Jack

He is a hard oak table, solid and reliable,
A gazelle running from its fierce predator in the 100m sprint,
He is a penalty box with fans cheering all around him,
A giant roar from the middle of nowhere,
A jolly morning that always has lots to say,
Jack.

Matthew Barnfield (9)
Warden Hill Primary School, Cheltenham

Seasons

Spring is like a glorious, tall sunflower
and a breeze with a tiny bit of power.

Summer is like a steam room, a huge ball of fire
although it's great to play in that I must admire.

Autumn is like a truck load of multicoloured stars
yet Hallowe'en is coming so we have a lot of chocolate bars.

Winter is like a beautiful snowflake gliding down to a puffy cloud
it slowly drifts upon the wind, it's not at all very loud.

That's all four seasons of the year
and I haven't got a favourite because I hold them all so dear!

Adam Hannis (9)
Warden Hill Primary School, Cheltenham

My Mum

She's a springy bed, rocking me to sleep,
She's a cheeky monkey, making me laugh at her jokes,
My mum is a dark cupboard closed at night,
She's a screeching bird, angry and cross, sending me to bed,
She is a bright sunset, ready to tuck me up in bed.

Millie Dawson (9)
Warden Hill Primary School, Cheltenham

My Dad

He is a wooden table with lots of legs.
My dad is a cheetah because he's quite fast at running
But he cheats at games.
He is Florida because he's always on about a holiday there.
He's definitely a quick noise because every day he's busy.
My dad is an afternoon because he is always peaceful.

Billy Wright (9)
Warden Hill Primary School, Cheltenham

My Dad

He's an office chair with pictures of me on it.
He's a door with a broken bike on the step.

He's a smart dog which will still eat anything.
He's a cat because he sleeps in at weekends.

My dad is like GCHQ 'cause he thinks he owns the place.
He's a garage, always open because he enjoys fixing bikes.

He's Queen's Greatest Hits in the cupboard.
He's the sound of a wrench whining.

He's tea time because he's always hungry.
He's 8 o'clock because it's my bed time.

Tom Williams (9)
Warden Hill Primary School, Cheltenham

My Dad

My dad is a new, bright blue, comfy sofa.
He is a friendly gorilla, never getting angry.
He is a brand new football pitch, waiting to get everybody
                                    into the seats.
He sounds like a rattle of shiny keys,
A crumpled chocolate wrapper rustling.
He is like the middle of the day, sun high in the sky, never giving up.

Ellen Pearce (9)
Warden Hill Primary School, Cheltenham

My Friend, Sam

He's a mantelpiece full of rugby medals.
He's a muddy field where he can practise his rugby.
He's a brave soldier fighting for his team.
He's a roaring lion, king of his pride.
He's up early in the morning, full of beans and ready to battle.

Matthew Armitage (9)
Warden Hill Primary School, Cheltenham

My Best Friend, Joe

He's a big, brand new, state of the art sofa, straight from the wrapper.
He's as fast as a peregrine falcon swooping down to catch its prey.
He never loses a race!
He's a superb goalkeeper who never lets in a goal!
The sound of a weird chuckle.
The sound of a zooming Ferrari speeding down an American highway.
The sound of a boy who never wants to get up.
A cracking goalkeeper.

Daniel Jacques (9)
Warden Hill Primary School, Cheltenham

My Mum

She's a big, soft, comfy bed waiting to comfort someone lying on her.
She's a pretty peacock showing off her lovely feathers.
She's the busy town with loads of people buying clothes.
She's the sound of boiling hot cooking pots in an oven inside
a nice warm kitchen.
She's the bright summer morning with the sun shining in through
the glistening window.

Joe Williams (9)
Warden Hill Primary School, Cheltenham

My Sister

She is a soft feather pillow so cuddly and warm.
She is a small prickly hedgehog hibernating in the winter under the
bright scarlet sky.
She is a meadow full of sweet-smelling flowers.
She is a little whistle coming from a nightingale.
She is summer because she is sunny, warm and welcoming,
My sister.

Jodie Cave (9)
Warden Hill Primary School, Cheltenham

My Friend

She's a comfy bed with olive-coloured wood.
She's a sparkly silver sofa with white patterns on it.
She's a tall giraffe with brown spots all over.
She's as quick as a peregrine falcon diving to catch her prey.
She's a field full of bright red poppies.
She's a parrot saying hello to a customer in the pet shop.
She's a warm summer's evening with birds fluttering
Across the sky making a chirping sound as they go.

Harriet Oddy (9)
Warden Hill Primary School, Cheltenham

My Brother, Jon

He is the morning when he's up, bright and ready for a
school day of work!
He is a flying, bouncy, inflatable chair, too bouncy to sit on!
He is a laughing kookaburra chuckling!
He is a bright, giggling monkey whom you'll never know
when he's going to pounce and tickle you!
He is the smell of Lynx deodorant!
He is a *joke* shop filled with loads of practical jokes, he uses
a lot at home!

Rebecca Faull (9)
Warden Hill Primary School, Cheltenham

My Friend, Roy

He is an old armchair with some stuffing falling out of an arm.
He is a worldly wise owl telling me lots of interesting facts.
He is the countryside because he is slow and quiet.
He is the sound of birds in the evening.
He is the warm summer's evening when everything slows down
and gets quieter.

Thomas Hayward (9)
Warden Hill Primary School, Cheltenham

My Mum

She is a super comfy bed with bright orange covers
Waiting for someone to sleep in it.

She is a springy kangaroo
Always doing useful things.

She is an appealing, fragranced kitchen
Cooking delicious food.

She is a flute playing tranquilly.

She is a calm night in wintertime
With snow falling lightly.

She is a bunch of roses
Just picked.

Iain Greig (9)
Warden Hill Primary School, Cheltenham

My Dad

He is an old, brown, spotty settee.
He is a bird swooping in the sky.
He is a house in the middle of Cheltenham.
He is a barking dog in a field.
He is a sunny day sitting on the beach
Watching the children playing on the beach digging holes.

Sam Godwin (9)
Warden Hill Primary School, Cheltenham

My Sister, Sarah

She is a comfy cabin-bed waiting to be snuggled up in.
She is a koala in a bamboo tree, chomping bamboo sticks slowly.
She is an ivy-covered cottage turning into a big blue mansion.
She sounds like a quiet ladybird waiting for the right moment to fly off.
She is a morning in spring waiting to get through the day to rest.

Cheryl Davies (9)
Warden Hill Primary School, Cheltenham

My Mum

She's like a newly delivered sofa
With a wonderful pattern

She's a newborn puppy
All playful and full of life

A garden centre in the spring
With all the blossom on the plants

A hanging chime gently blowing in the wind
Then getting louder

She's a summer evening
Warm and bright

She smells like fresh roses in our garden!

Rachael Carruthers (9)
Warden Hill Primary School, Cheltenham

My Friend

He is a blue cushion, staying by your side.
He is a tiny mouse always sneaking around.
He is a spy, always in the right place when you need him.
He is a quiet ant, scurrying and not making a sound.
He is summer at the time when men go out and sunbathe.

Sam Holdaway (9)
Warden Hill Primary School, Cheltenham

My Dad

He is a comfy bed because when you lie on him he is very comfy.
He is a dog because he barks suddenly.
He is a busy town because he is always moving.
He is the sound of cars snarling because he is talking all the time.
He is the time of morning because he is always the first one up.

Jake Rostron (9)
Warden Hill Primary School, Cheltenham

My Friend

She's a warm comfy bed with gold stars on the duvet.
She's a colourful armchair with stripes on it.
She's a spotty hyena because she laughs all the time.
She's a cheeky monkey swinging from classroom to classroom.
She's a clear blue swimming pool about to do a dive.
She's the sound of a violin playing a tune.
She's a cool breezy evening admiring the smell of roses.

Poppie Compton (9)
Warden Hill Primary School, Cheltenham

My Little Sister

My sister's a little cheerful girl
Because she's always happy
My sister lives in a busy whirl
In our whizzy family

She is brighter than the sun
Because she is very light
She brings me lots of fun
Because she is funny at night.

Natasha Goodwin (9)
Warden Hill Primary School, Cheltenham

Friends

F orever we shall be friends
R ight 'til the very end
I will always be there for you
E very moment of the day
N o one can break our friendship, no matter how they try
D epending on each other, it's what we like to do
S o that's what friends are for.

Lauren Greville (9)
Warden Hill Primary School, Cheltenham

If I Were An Animal

If I were a kangaroo,
I would
Jump, jump, jump
All day long.
If I were a dolphin,
I would
Swim, swim, swim
Like mad
Or maybe a panther.

If I were a rabbit,
I would
Hop, hop, hop
Everywhere.
If I were a snake,
I would
Slither, slither, slither
All the time
Or a dog,
I do not know,
Which would you be?

Hannah Jones (8)
Westbury Park Primary School, Bristol

Is It A Dream?

Today I saw a monkey
Climbing up a tree
He had big brown eyes
A very strong tail
I said, 'Don't follow me'

Then I saw an elephant
Walking by a stream
He had two big ears
A very long trunk
I thought it was a dream.

Jessica Bell (8)
Westbury Park Primary School, Bristol

Octopus

As the octopus' long wavy tentacles
Spread out to reach its babies,
The fish back away,
The orange bumpy octopus
Slowly sneaks through the coral-covered reef,
The octopus stays as still as an ancient rock
In its dark inky hole,
When the swordfish approaches
It squirts a cloud of angry jet-black ink.

Hannah Brindle (8)
Westbury Park Primary School, Bristol

Spiders

I sat up in bed in the middle of the night,
I sat frozen at a horrible sight,
Eight long legs crept round my door
And then it scuttled along the floor,
Its body was the size of a black tennis ball,
It has scared me and it would scare all,
Big black spider go away,
Don't come back another day.

Cecily Bain (8)
Westbury Park Primary School, Bristol

Guess Who?

Swimming and jumping is my thing
We love listening to people sing
We hate to hear people cry
So we will give a great sigh
I am the dolphin.

Abigael Brain (8)
Westbury Park Primary School, Bristol

My Favourite Animal

He's grey, as grey as a tabletop,
He's fat, as fat as an elephant,
His tail is shorter than short,
He loves his mud baths,
He never eats fish,
He smells quite bad,
His eyes gleam in the sun,
Have you guessed it?
Yes, it's a *hippo!*

Fleur Sainsbury (10)
Westbury Park Primary School, Bristol

The Elephant

It lives in Africa and India,
It has big ears to hear with,
It is very big,
They try to kill them for their tusks
That are made out of ivory,
When they have babies
The babies hold the mummy's tail with their trunk,
They use their trunk for drinking and picking up food.

Isabel Avery (8)
Westbury Park Primary School, Bristol

Zebras

Z igzag stripes, white and black.
E ating golden grass as a snack.
B lack and bristly, bushy mane.
R acing across the African plain.
A mazing animal, big and strong.
S wishes its long tail all day long.

Lauren Cuttell (8)
Westbury Park Primary School, Bristol

What Am I?

I am an animal
That scuttles from hole to hole
Like a thin, slithery stick,
With short, tiny, pointy feet.

I live in holes in the rocks,
The colour of my skin is either green or red,
I play in the hot weather with my friends.

In hot places I mostly live,
I hide in little places in walls,
My animal name begins with L.

Can you guess what I am?
A lizard!

Ella Jones (8)
Westbury Park Primary School, Bristol

Dogs, Dogs And More Dogs

Dogs are yellow, gold and brown,
They all like fooling around,
They're all nice and cuddly,
They're all cute and lovely,
When they are puppies they drink milk
And feel as soft as silk,
They like a good home
And a fat, juicy bone,
They like a long walk
And they listen when I talk,
Dogs are so good,
I've loved them since my childhood,
Dogs are so great!

Celia Johnson-Morgan (8)
Westbury Park Primary School, Bristol

Penguins

I am an expert swimmer
I skim across the water
Chasing fish and squids
My home is icy cold
And polar bears are my neighbours
My beak and wings are small
And I waddle from side to side
Can you guess who I am?
Before I go for a slide
I am a penguin.

Kamarl Rauf (8)
Westbury Park Primary School, Bristol

Frogs

They are cold to the touch, like ice,
They sit in the shadow of the giant leaves
That to them look like trees,
From the circle of life
And the short cold life,
Under the leaves wet and dripping
Slurping up bugs and flies.

Emily Bull (8)
Westbury Park Primary School, Bristol

Tigers

Some people think they are scary killers
But I think they are so cute
Because their red fur looks like fire
Their black fur is as dark as the midnight sky
Their noses are so shiny, they look like a new button
Their eyes sparkle like a new sun.

Jocelyn Eccles (8)
Westbury Park Primary School, Bristol

Spiders

Spiders, spiders
Orange and black
Some of them thin
Some of them fat
Some of them sporty
Full of breath
Others lazy just like the cat.

Flora Jetha (8)
Westbury Park Primary School, Bristol

Predators

Scaly, smooth and rough
As he stalks his prey
Slowly goes a bit closer
The coloured pattern of his skin
Will keep predators away
Sudden movement . . .
What is he?

Lois Barton (8)
Westbury Park Primary School, Bristol

Dolphins

Lovely silvery-blue,
Gliding amongst the waves,
Then you see a glimpse of blue,
It's a dolphin twirling in mid-air,
Suddenly it's gone back into the water,
Sitting on the edge of the sea,
Watching the amazing animals play.

Emily Staricoff (8)
Westbury Park Primary School, Bristol

The Hairdresser

I went to the hairdresser today,
She was very kind to me,
She had hair as tidy as shampoo bottles
And skin very pale like the tea she serves,
That smile, I know that smile.

I went to the hairdresser today,
She was very nice to me,
She was as quick as an electric hairdryer,
Her earrings were as bright as mirrors,
That smile, I know that smile.

I went to the hairdresser today,
She was truly kind to me,
Skin as smooth as leathery seats,
Eyes sparkling like brand new sinks
And that smile, I know that smile . . .
It was a hairbrush!

Jasmine Taylor (11)
Westbury Park Primary School, Bristol

Who Am I?

You're small and very tiny
And live in little holes,
Your whiskers always twitching
Beside your pinky nose.

Some people think you're scary
But I think you're quite sweet,
As soon as I look down
You're just above my feet!

You scuttle along the table
With your little paws,
To you we are giants
And to us you're so small!

Monica Lindsay-Perez (8)
Westbury Park Primary School, Bristol

The Snowman

I have two big black eyes,
They are the shape of pies.

The orange thing upon my nose,
Is used for something no one knows!

I have a big black scarf,
It's wrapped around my neck

And when it starts to strange me,
I go, 'Oh heck!'

The sun is coming out,
I'm just about to melt.

My last few words are bread and jelly,
That's what I had for brunch.

I'm starting to get dizzy,
The sun is really hot.

The sun is burning my little brother
And his name is Pop.

I'm now a puddle on the ground,
Spring has come this way.

I'm just about to disappear,
Olé, olé, olé!

Safiya Bashir (10)
Westbury Park Primary School, Bristol

Cats

Some cats are fluffy, small and cuddly,
Sometimes they act quite funny,
They can sometimes be the colour of grey,
Or even sometimes the colour of hay,
Their ears prick up like the end of a pencil,
They listen when I talk and go out for long walks,
Cats, cats, cats!

Rachel Bews (8)
Westbury Park Primary School, Bristol

Winnie The Pooh Likes Honey

Winnie the Pooh likes honey,
He said that to his tummy.

Piglet thought it was funny,
While he was counting money.

Tigger likes bouncing
And he likes pouncing.

Eeyore looked at Tigger's stripes
And then he finished counting pipes!

Rabbit likes carrots
And he dreams of turning into a parrot!

Owl is very weird,
But he doesn't have a beard!

When Kanga is jumping,
She makes a loud thumping.

Roo likes hopping in the sand,
While listening to her favourite band.

They're all the very best of friends
And their friendship will *never* end!

Natalie Oxford & Charlotte Moran (10)
Westbury Park Primary School, Bristol

Animals

A naconda are a type of snake.
N ile crocodiles live in lakes.
I nsects can be quite scary.
M ammoths were quite hairy.
A nimals are very cute.
L izards are similar to newts.
S nails are not very cute.

Clemency Carroll (8)
Westbury Park Primary School, Bristol

Penguin

The penguin waddles up to shore,
It dives in deep,
Swirling around,
In the icy cold water.

As it swims,
In the deep,
Catching fish,
Through and through.

Then climbs back up,
As before
And heads for its snowy cave,
To feed its babies.

It slips and slithers
On the icy bank,
Its flippers very clumsy,
Tripping over each other.

As it enters the cave,
A noise,
It's gone,
Out of sight.

It peeks out,
The danger is gone,
They are safe,
The babies cheep.

Mum penguin drops the food down,
Tears it up
And gives
To babies.

Mum goes back out,
Swimming
And sliding,
Her same routine.

Zoe Rasbash (8)
Westbury Park Primary School, Bristol

The Dentist

Today the dentist said to me,
'Your teeth are stained with tea.'
When she smiled I noticed that
Her snowy-white teeth glowed.

Today the dentist said to me,
'Your teeth look the colour of kiwi.'
As she moved around the surgery
I noticed that she was
As energetic as an electric toothbrush.

Today the dentist said to me,
'Your teeth are the colour of green tea.'
As I looked around the room
It was as clean as a whistle.

Today the dentist said to me,
'Your teeth are the colour of broccoli.'
As she bent down to check my mouth,
Her breath was as fresh as a minty mouthwash.

Today the dentist said to me,
'Yippy, your teeth are clean!'

Millie Snook (11)
Westbury Park Primary School, Bristol

Policeman

Equipment as strong as he is,
A hat as big as his head,
His legs as long as a giraffe's neck
And runs as fast as a prison gate closing on you.

He is as smart as his suit,
His baton flicks out like a spring,
He is as huge as a bouncer
And runs so fast, like a cheetah.

Thomas Hellin (10)
Westbury Park Primary School, Bristol

The Greengrocer

Miss Marie is a greengrocer,
Her eyes are broccoli green,
Every day and every night,
She does a little clean.

Miss Marie is a greengrocer,
Her smile as wide as pepper strips,
Every day and every night,
She always has a trip.

Miss Marie is a greengrocer,
Her cheeks as red as tomatoes,
Every day and every night,
She sits down and sews.

Miss Marie is a greengrocer,
Now happily retired,
Her shop is on the market,
Waiting to be hired.

Tilly Maidment-Otlet (10)
Westbury Park Primary School, Bristol

Kittens

Kittens are warm and cuddly,
they drink lots of bubbly.
They sleep by the fire,
not near the electric wire.

They play all night
and never fight.
They've got soft fur
and they like to purr.

Kittens are very small,
they like to climb the wall.
They drink out of the sink,
then they give you a wink.

Jessie Moran (8)
Westbury Park Primary School, Bristol

The Nightmare

When little Jimmy Thomas said,
'Mother, don't make me go to bed
It scares me so
It really does.'
His mother simply said,
'Tut tut' and 'Nonsense, dear.'
And, 'If you go to bed you will not hear
The noises that go round and round
Up in the air
And on the ground.'

When these words were out of her mouth
Little Jimmy's blood ran cold
He said, 'Oh Mother please describe these sounds
The ones that go round and round
The new ones and the old . . .'

His mother said, 'That will not do
If I did, your bones would rattle
Your spine would shiver
Your teeth chatter . . .'

All that night there was not a peep
From little Jimmy fast asleep
But inside his head things weren't so clever
He had his worst nightmare ever!

Elsa Andreski (10)
Westbury Park Primary School, Bristol

Hunting

The dark, menacing, orange tarantula,
The startling of light shone on its bared teeth,
Thick, green, silhouetted trees tower over the little spider,
A rustling noise began then out popped a fly buzzing by,
It suddenly pounced on the tiny fly,
There's a deathly silence while it devours its prey.

Daniel Cullum (8)
Westbury Park Primary School, Bristol

The Florist

Miss Muffet is a florist,
With cheeks red as a rose,
She sells all kinds of garden things,
Like spades, forks and hoes.

Miss Muffet is a florist,
Eyes the colour of bluebells,
Cards and toys and flowers
Are among the things she sells.

Miss Muffet is a florist,
Her teeth - they're shining white,
Exactly the colour of snowdrops,
When they are in sight.

Miss Muffet is a florist,
Hair curly as a bamboo shoot,
Her favourite plant is a magnolia tree,
Outside the shop that's taken root.

Miss Muffet is a florist,
Eyes brighter than sunflowers,
The real ones in her garden
Are taller than towers!

Miss Muffet is a florist,
Sweet as a forget-me-not,
Her hands are butter fingers,
Every day she breaks a pot!

Esmé Bain (11)
Westbury Park Primary School, Bristol

Greasy Teen

That greasy kid in the burger bar,
He gives me all my change,
Slops the burger in the bun
And cooks it on the range.

That greasy kid in the burger bar,
He yells my order to his lord,
High-pitched voice,
Like nails down the board.

That greasy kid in the burger bar,
Mops the floor 'til you could slip,
Sniffs and coughs and mops his brow,
For he's as gangly as a drooping chip.

That greasy kid in the burger bar,
Oh he's a right one,
Tall and thin and still at school,
As spotty as a sesame bun.

That greasy kid in the burger bar,
He's got no hope that man,
He's young and thin and his hair's
As greasy as a frying pan.

That greasy kid in the burger bar,
He's got such an ugly mug,
Dark, hooded eyes like drive-through windows
And scurries like a discovered bug.

That greasy kid in the burger bar,
He looks like such a brat,
But in my heart I love him,
He's my brother and a great one at that!

Sean Jamshidi (11)
Westbury Park Primary School, Bristol

Where Little Angels Care To Tread

With angels in the cloudy heights,
The foggy little clowns,
Along there came an ugly one,
That sent the skylarks down.

Now looks can be deceptive
And this is widely known,
Where little angels care to tread,
This cherub would have flown.

The moral of this story,
A piece of great advice,
Never judge an angel by its wings,
They may be nice.

Nicola Papastavrou Brooks (10)
Westbury Park Primary School, Bristol

The Pirate

A pirate's eyes are as black as an eye patch,
A face as scarred as his ship.

A pirate be as strong as an anchor,
Sharp as his cutlass blade.

A pirate be as fit as a cabin boy,
Powerful as a cannonball.

A pirate be sturdy as a mast,
He hopes to get some plunder,
Yaarr!

Rose Ireland (11)
Westbury Park Primary School, Bristol

The Grocery Lady

As sour as a blackberry,
Voice as sharp as a lemon,
Eyes like green gooseberries.

Through the window her eyes
Are sharp as she looks at me.

Cheeks as red as a tomato,
Teeth like little chunks of pineapple,
Fingernails as long and pointed as carrots.

Through the window her face is stern
As she glares at me.

So now every time I walk past her shop,
I duck down so that she cannot see me.

Georgie Hope (10)
Westbury Park Primary School, Bristol

The Baker

I go to the baker's every Monday,
I see his face as round as a currant bun,
I see his eyes, two small currants,
I see his mouth, a curving croissant.

I go to the baker's every Tuesday,
I see his belly as a white bread roll,
I see his heart as soft as a raw gingerbread man,
I see his fingers, two fat chocolate éclairs.

I go to the baker's every Wednesday,
I see his ears, two big fat doughnuts,
He's as big as the big baking tray,
His feet are like two big chocolate bars.

Jade Hellin (10)
Westbury Park Primary School, Bristol

The Secretary

I broke the phone today
She'll treat me like a mouse
She'll be like a ray of fire
She'll tell my mum in the house.

I broke the phone today
Her eyes will be like red pins
I'm doomed forever
I can see her eyes spin.

I broke the phone today
Her hair will steam as black as the phone
I can see detention
I'll be just skin and bone.

I broke the phone today
Her dress as blue as ink will crease
My face will go red
I'm sweating like grease.

I broke the phone today
Her shoes as brown as the desk will stamp
I feel sick
I've broken the lamp.

Alice Dale (10)
Westbury Park Primary School, Bristol

The Soldier's Eye

Inside the soldier's eye, an endless war
Inside the endless war, a soldier's hatred
Inside the soldier's hatred, a million deaths
Inside the million deaths, a soldier's blood
Inside the soldier's blood, a broken heart
Inside the broken heart, a soldier's tear
Inside the soldier's tear, a blood-red poppy
Inside the blood-red poppy, a soldier's eye.

Tom Last (9)
Westbury Park Primary School, Bristol

The Nightmare

In the night you're upstairs,
Twisting and turning in your bed,
When creeping upstairs,
Heading to make its cobweb,
Is your worst nightmare,
Yes, you guessed right,
It was a gigantic tarantula.
Quick, covers across your head,
Grab a torch, hide, quickly inside your den,
This is what you thought,
Just over the covers that are on your head,
Is the cobweb that you dread!
Too scared to run,
Too terrified to move,
When that spider starts its search for *food!*
Then, in the next room I hear a scream,
I dash in and guess what I see?
Yes, me, dead on the floor of my mum and dad's room,
What happened?

Emily Jennings & Rianna Newman (8)
West Town Lane Junior School, Brislington

Zoe's Zoo

In her zoo, Zoe kept . . .
Ten cows that moo powerfully and stand there all day eating grass
Nine pigs that are fat and snort noisily
Eight hares that run fiercely
Seven horses that eat hay madly
Six budgies that bite hard
Five frogs that jump in the pond with a big splash
Four snakes that slither sidewards
Three dolphins that jump right up from the waves
Two pigs that race one another
And one . . . guess what?

Kayleigh Sims (8)
West Town Lane Junior School, Brislington

Poison Potion

Rat's head,
Slimy bed,
Guts of snake,
With a mouldy cake.

Wing of bat,
Tail of cat.

Double, double,
I'm in trouble,
Blood bubble,
Cauldron rubble.

Old man's toe,
Slimy bow,
With bogey dough.

Donkey's brain,
Smelliest drain,
Mixed with,
The worst pain.

Rat's tail,
Garbage pale,
Liver of pig,
Guts of earwig.

Double, double,
I'm in trouble,
Blood bubble,
Cauldron rubble.

Horse's eye,
Liver pie,
Blood tie.

Toe of dragon,
Monkey brain,
With a ghost train.

Goat tongue,
Elephant dung.

Now it's ready,
Serve steady.

Michael Dyer (10)
West Town Lane Junior School, Brislington

Five Little Cats

Said the first little cat
With a quick little hum,
'I wish I could find
A kind little mum.'

Said the second little cat
With a quick little pat,
'I wish I could find
A fat little bat.'

Said the third little cat
With a quick little call,
'I wish I could find
A nice, juicy ball.'

Said the fourth little cat
With a quick little bellow,
'I wish I could find
The colour yellow!'

Said the fifth little cat
With a quick lie,
I wish I could say
Goodbye!'

Ashley Lewis (8)
West Town Lane Junior School, Brislington

School

Head teacher, head teacher,
You're the boss, you're the boss.
Head teacher, head teacher,
You're the one who rules the school.

Teachers, teachers,
Tell you off if you are naughty.
Teachers, teachers,
Give you homework every week.

Children, children,
Better be good and never naughty.
Children, children,
No kicking and never punch.

Now keep this poem in your mind,
Then the teachers may be kind.

Adrienne Day (9)
West Town Lane Junior School, Brislington

Three Little Cats

Said the first little cat
With a quick little scratch,
'I wish I could find
A fat little match.'

Said the second little cat
With a slightly small miaow,
'I wish I could find
A fat little cow.'

Said the third little cat
With a small, small sniff,
'I wish I could find
A small little whiff!'

Lauren Payne (8)
West Town Lane Junior School, Brislington

A Spooky Spell!

Eye of newt, brains of dog,
A spice of chilli legs of frog.

A litre of blood, a touch of venom,
A head of a cow with a slice of lemon.

Scale of dragon, a howlet's wing,
Wool of bat, a hornet's sting.

Double, double, toil and trouble,
Fire burn, cauldron bubble.

Witches' mums in the dark,
A rat's tail, a salted sea shark.

Double, double, toil and trouble,
Fire burn, cauldron bubble.

A pot of snot, an eye of cat,
A monkey's ear, tail of rat,
Mix it well, stir it up,
Blood and mud in a mouldy cup.

Conner Neale (10)
West Town Lane Junior School, Brislington

Zoe's Zoo

In her zoo Zoe kept . . .
Ten elephants that stomped around their cage,
Nine lions that roared in the night,
Eight spiders that spun their webs,
Seven snakes that slithered on the ground,
Six sheep eating grass
Five rabbits that nibbled on their cage,
Four frogs that gulped at the flies,
Three rats that scrambled in the darkness,
Two hamsters that snored in the daylight
And one . . . guess what?

Daisy Pearce-Lyons (8)
West Town Lane Junior School, Brislington

Five Little Mice

Said the first little mouse
With a quick little tease,
'I wish I could find
A fat little piece of cheese.'

Said the second little mouse
With a quick little shriek,
'I wish I could find
Something to eat.'

Said the third little mouse
With a quick little yawn,
'I wish I could find
A fat little piece of corn.'

Said the fourth little mouse
With a quick little cry,
'I wish I could find
A nice, juicy fly.'

Said the fifth little mouse
With a quick little shrug,
'I wish I could find
A fat little baby slug.'

Chloe Little (8)
West Town Lane Junior School, Brislington

Stars

I never miss the stars above,
They are my only real love,
I dream all day and then at night,
I dream of what it must be like,
To be up there, to see the world asleep and winding by,
But when the clouds cover the sky,
I feel like something's just not right,
But then to my delight they come back in sight.

Samantha Jones (10)
West Town Lane Junior School, Brislington

Poison Bubbling

Ibble obble chocolate bubble
Poison bubbling
Toil and trouble

A leg of a newt, an eye of a frog,
A wing of a bat, a tongue of a dog,
A crocodile's fork, a blind bee's sting,
A dog's leg and a blackbird's wing.

A head of a monkey, a leg of a snake,
An eye of a dog, in a river lake,
A witch's nose, a blind man's wig,
A horse's eyeball and a big fat pig.

A hamster's head, a cow's liver,
A cat's leg and it makes me shiver,
So now I will say goodbye today,
Ready to come another day.

Grace Haines (10)
West Town Lane Junior School, Brislington

Dragon

On the cloud I see its scales, purple and green,
It glares at me looking mean,
A shade of red fire flickers out its mouth.

It zooms through the air,
With beady red eyes,
It glares at me, it's so big in size,
My heart is pounding as it gets closer.

On its glittery green back I leap,
Soaring through the sky,
I feel like I could fly.
I flew away to a faraway land
And I was never seen again.

Abby Hoyle (10)
West Town Lane Junior School, Brislington

The Cauldron

Boil it, stir it, mix it round,
Keep the bubbles going down,
In the cauldron boil and bake,
There's no time to make mistakes.

Cat's paw, a bat's wing,
A lion's roar, an adder's sting,
Pig's eye and tongue of dog,
A devil's fire, the skin of a frog.

Boil it, stir it, mix it round,
Keep the bubbles going down,
In the cauldron boil and bake,
There's no time to make mistakes.

A pig's bladder, sheep's bones,
Kingfisher's beak and dragon's moan,
Lion's heart, slug's trail,
Lizard's leg and a squished snail.

Emma Brown (10)
West Town Lane Junior School, Brislington

Sam The Horse

As I gallop through the fields,
Happiness and joy spreads around me,
People ride me every day
And like me all the same way,
Happiness and joy spreads around me,
While people love me,
Other horses have their fun
And play with me all day long,
Every horse wants people,
They like to be ridden by all of them
And have happy times together,
To be friends.

Conor Woods (8)
West Town Lane Junior School, Brislington

Boil And Bake!

Stir, mix, taste, shake,
All the things to boil and bake.

A dog's bark, an elephant's trunk,
A crow's clark, a hairy punk.
A sting of a bee, a cat's lip,
A hot cup of tea, a mouldy chip

Stir, mix, taste, shake,
All the things to boil and bake.

Ink of a pen, three lumps of cheese,
A wing of a hen and a very big sneeze.
A pencil lead, a pig's heart,
A rabbit's ear, a mouldy tart.
A gold tooth, a snake's bite,
An old grandad, a big bad fight.

Stir, mix, taste, shake,
All the things to boil and bake.

Laura McEllin (11)
West Town Lane Junior School, Brislington

Zoe's Zoo

In her zoo, Zoe kept . . .
Ten snakes that slither all day long.
Nine monkeys swinging on the bars.
Eight tigers scratching on the old tree.
Seven lazy crocodiles walking along the bridge.
Six ducks swimming in the old lake.
Five lizards climbing the tall tree.
Four birds flying up and down in the sky.
Three sandcats climbing over the rocks.
Two goldfish swimming around
And *one . . . guess what?*

Isabella Broome (9)
West Town Lane Junior School, Brislington

Double, Double, Toil And Trouble

Double, double, toil and trouble
Fire burn and cauldron bubble

Juicy, juicy, slimy frogs
Burning ashes, blackened logs
Smelly stinking foul feet
Pig's ears piled very neat
Smelly, welly, dog's breath
Cow's belly leads to death

Double, double, toil and trouble
Fire burn and cauldron bubble

Squeaking, scratching rat tails
Sizzle it up with the slime of snails
Dragon spit, monkey's brain
Snot of a tiger, lion's mane
Gooey, gooey rhino's phlegm
Now chuck in a water hen

Double, double, toil and trouble
Fire burn and cauldron bubble.

Daniel Griffin (10)
West Town Lane Junior School, Brislington

Witch's Trouble

Double, double, toil and trouble,
Bubble, bubble, witch's trouble.

Ferret stew and hair of hare,
Smelly loos and foot of bear.

Eye of fish, guts of rat,
Earwax dish and eye of cat.

Toe of giant, smell of rat,
Smelly pigs and a lump of fat.

Hairy warts and maggot stew,
Faggots with a cow's moo.

Jack Rogers (11)
West Town Lane Junior School, Brislington

Night-Time

At night you can watch the stars shine
So magically-coloured
The moon twinkles beyond
So far in space
The night sets its magic on you
The cats go on a night-time walk
Silently creeping out
Balancing on the wall, cats mating
Swiftly the glittery moon lights the sky
Night-time business
Stars so glittery
The moon their master
Stars singing and dancing for the moon
Sparkle . . . twinkle all night long.

Lydia Hughes (8)
West Town Lane Junior School, Brislington

My Cauldron

Double, double, toil and trouble,
Miss Upton's head and cauldron bubble,
A school chair and rat's guts,
A grizzly bear and salted peanuts,
Lion's tail and guts of a snail
And then add a stinky toenail,
Double, double, toil and trouble,
A tiger's tail and a head of a snail,
A monkey's brain and an engine of a train,
My mum's hair and Tony Blair.

Double, double, toil and trouble,
Miss Upton's head and cauldron bubble,
A school chair and rat's guts,
A grizzly bear and salted peanuts.

Jack Bostock (10)
West Town Lane Junior School, Brislington

Witches' Potion

Lots of bogeys from the tin
Garbage from the little bin
Bear's blood all covered in poo
Zebra's dead body that's from the zoo
Dead man's toe and heart of a rat
Brain of a rat and eye of bat

Double, double, toil and trouble
Fire burn and cauldron bubble

Rat's tail all covered in dirt
A smelly dress from a lady who flirts
Dead man's head and rotten ear
Flesh of a new and gone-off bear
Cat's fat, nice slimy blood of a man
Woman's hand cut off by a fan

Double, double, toil and trouble
Fire burn, cauldron bubble.

Daisy Jones (10)
West Town Lane Junior School, Brislington

Witch's Cauldron

Rotten rat's blood and bat burgers,
Smelly socks and scary spiders.

A bag of change and a lot of oil,
Cauldron fill up and boil.

A sparkle of light, give me a fright,
A cow's tongue and a great big fight.

An eye of a shark,
A hairy dog's bark.

A pushbike, a flash of thunder,
A snake of fright, fall and lumber.

Rotten rat's blood and bat burgers,
Smelly socks and scary spiders.

Liam Plumpton (11)
West Town Lane Junior School, Brislington

Witch's Poem

Crust of a bogey, ear of a pig
Pop of a wart, old smelly wig
Pinch of earwax, mush of peas
Nose of a man, 500 fleas
Smell of bird's poo, orange tiger stripe
Moany neighbours, rat poison pipe

Double, double, toil and trouble
Fire burn and cauldron bubble

Scream of a child, smelly egg
Sand in cuts and pirate's leg
Slime of a snail, witch's breath
Claws of rat, bit of Black Death
Mushy, damp, mud, gangrened foot
Corpse's eyeball, bag of soot

Double, double, toil and trouble
Fire burn, cauldron bubble.

Bethany Cooper (10)
West Town Lane Junior School, Brislington

The Cauldron

Double, double, toil and trouble,
Fire burn, cauldron bubble.

Guts of rat, snail's shell,
Eyes which look like they're from Hell,
A slug's head, squelchy earwax,
Maggots' legs and giant bats.

Double, double, toil and trouble,
Fire burn, cauldron bubble.

A slimy snail shell and dog's fur,
A pig's gut and a cat's purr.

A dog's ear and fish blood,
A rat's tongue and stinky mud.

Thomas Edwards (10)
West Town Lane Junior School, Brislington

Boil, Boil In A Pot

Boil, boil in a pot
Mix it up with a load of snot
Piggy, piggy, nasty bladder
Stir it up with a rusty ladder
An icky brain from monkey stew
Mix it up with a stinky shoe
Sticky whale's eyes mixed with a tongue
Then throw in a load of dung
It is getting really nasty
It's nothing like a Cornish pasty
Boil, boil in a pot
Mix it up with a load of snot
Now it's time for tiger tails
Add in some of my mum's long nails
I like it when we use some blood
We even add a brown old scud
A rhino eye and a bull's grey horn
Then shake in a can of corn
Boil, boil in a pot
Mix it up with a load of snot!

Tom Payne (10)
West Town Lane Junior School, Brislington

The Cauldron

Double, double, toil and trouble
Fire burn and cauldron bubble

Bogeys in cups, a monkey's brain
Feet of ducks, a lion's mane

Slime of snail, eye of bat
Arm of cat, tail of rat

Double, double, toil and trouble
Fire burn and cauldron bubble

My mum's earwax, tiger's heart
My dad's mouldy flan, skateboard from Bart!

Alice Gregory (10)
West Town Lane Junior School, Brislington

My Poison Pot!

Rough stuff, marrow of bone,
Clouds of blood and sweltered stone,
Tail of snake, pink pig's snout,
Muck of cows and scale from trout,
Head lice crawling around my pot,
Mix it together and there's my lot.

Double, double, toil and trouble,
Fire burn and cauldron bubble.

Smelly sweat from old armpits,
A dirty face with spots and zits,
Cuts and scabs plus gruel and grime,
Tattered, battered rags of slime,
Sick and vomit mixed with mud,
A bald man's feet, skin and chud,
A sick skunk's smell with sewers and drains,
Loch Ness' teeth and monster's veins.

Eleanor Baldock (10)
West Town Lane Junior School, Brislington

My Potion

Eye of a cat, skin of a snake
The smell of a 50-year-old hat
A cat's eye and the guts of a rat
Freshly squeezed with a wing of a bat
Hair of a brain and bloody rain

Double, double, toil and bubble
Fire burn, cauldron bubble
Brains of a bat with a hairless cat
Wings of a gnat and a dead man's hat
Double, double, toil and bubble
Fire burn, cauldron bubble.

Matthew Flook (10)
West Town Lane Junior School, Brislington

Macbeth

Double, double, toil and trouble,
Fire burn and cauldron bubble
All the things I've got in my pot,
I have dead animals, I've got,
Baking hot eye of fish,
Red-hot on my dish,
Warty toad's slimy skin,
A fish's scale,
An end of a pin,
The patterned shell of a snail,
A big brown water pail.
Chorus
Long tongues of snakes,
My pot boils and bakes,
A brown dog's loud bark,
An owl that's in the dark,
A lion's huge big head,
A big bouncy bed.
Chorus
A big mouldy jelly,
My friend's hairy belly,
A cow's moo,
My nan's loo.
Chorus.

Chloe Jenkins (10)
West Town Lane Junior School, Brislington

Hoth And Throth

Hoth and throth, bubble broth,
Turning, burning, hoth and throth.

Snake vomit, snail shell,
Boiled in a dusty cell.

Hoth and throth, bubble broth,
Turning, burning, hoth and troth.

Eagle wing, throat of frog,
Octopus blood, ear of dog.

Hoth and throth, bubble broth,
Turning, burning, hoth and throth.

Orange acid, guts of slug,
Harpie's feather, fresh ground bug.

Hoth and throth, bubble broth,
Turning, burning, hoth and throth.

Moonlight stream, tornado air,
Trapped inside a box with care.

Hoth and throth, bubble broth,
Turning, burning, hoth and throth.

Black clam shell, bat eyelid,
The longest tentacle of a giant squid.

Hoth and throth, bubble broth,
Turning, burning, hoth and throth.

Dino Carobene (10)
West Town Lane Junior School, Brislington

Witches' Poem

Beak of eagle, fin of shark
Pool of murk and wing of skylark
Tooth of tiger, eyeballs on a dish
Pit of slime and sting of a jellyfish
Gone-off cheese, pit of gunk
Heart of snail and scent of skunk

Double, double, toil and trouble
Fire burn and cauldron bubble

Legs of cat, slime of slug
Fang of bat and eyes in a mug
Eyes of spider, foot of bat
Flesh-eating scarabs and fur of rat
Mummy's curse, eye of creep
Horse's shoe and foot of sheep

Double, double, toil and trouble
Fire burn and cauldron bubble

Eye of fly, heart of bat
Bite of dog and claw of cat
Horn of rhino, tooth of hog
Ear of rabbit and leap of frog
Whiskers of mouse, tongue of lizard
Tail of crocodile, magic of wizard

Double, double, toil and trouble
Fire burn and cauldron bubble.

Corrie Rose (10)
West Town Lane Junior School, Brislington

Things

Strawberries, bananas, apples and grapes,
Elephants, giraffes, monkeys and apes,
Red, yellow, purple and green,
They're the nicest things I've seen.

Eyeshadow, lipgloss and mascara too,
Coughs, colds and the flu,
Butterflies, ladybirds, bees and flies,
Mouths, ears, noses and eyes.

Literacy, numeracy, spellings and art,
Arms, legs, head and heart,
Biscuits, squash, drinks and food,
Lots of people have different moods.

Schools, teachers, pupils and work,
Cups, plates, knives and forks,
Tidy, messy, dirty and clean,
Kind, sad, healthy and mean.

Shoes, clothes, handbags and skirts,
When they see boys, girls will flirt,
Pop music and lots of tunes,
Fish, tuna and some prunes.

England, Ireland, Scotland, Wales,
Every fish has a tail,
Japan, China and Canada too,
There's lots of countries like Timbuktu!

Jessica Randall (9)
West Town Lane Junior School, Brislington

The Witch's Poem

An astronaut from outer space
With his snot and sweat from the race
Blood of a human and pus of a spot
Fag of a bat and an aftershot
A punch of a boxer and a bee's sting
A mummy's eye and a powerful wing

Double, double, toil and trouble
Fire burn and cauldron bubble

A big slam of a door and a girl's hat
Heart of a man, tongue of a cat
A smelly stream with lots of rats
Two lungs and a dirty old cat
A girl with fags who needs a good wash
Big human heart and people all squashed

Double, double, toil and trouble
Fire burn and cauldron bubble.

Sian Purnell (10)
West Town Lane Junior School, Brislington

Cauldron From Hell

A tail of a newt, an eye of a cat
A tongue of a fish, a wing of a bat
A leg of a frog under a log
An old, snotty, mouldy, old dog
Adder's fork, tongue from dog
An eye from a maggot, leg from a frog
Double, double, toil and trouble
Fire burning, cauldron bubble

Eye from a pig, sheep bones
Lion mane and teacher moan
Kingfisher head, lion's heart
A pencil lead, poisonous dart.

Sam Hanks (10)
West Town Lane Junior School, Brislington

Black Magic

Blood of vampire, skin of frog,
Misty magic from the fog,
Pink intestines of a pig,
Snail slime and an earwig,
Ghostly magic, a rat's tail,
Salt of sea, tongue of whale.

Dark underground, dug down deep,
Dark, damp dungeons horribly reek,
Magic words of disgusting choice,
Cackled with a croaky voice.

Mouldy jelly, chicken claws,
Crusty dandruff, veggie balls,
Sick of child, rabbit meat,
Stale spit and smelly feet.

Dark underground, dug down deep,
Dark, damp dungeons horribly reek,
Magic words of disgusting choice,
Cackled with a croaky voice.

Stir the mixture, mix it well,
Finish with a magic spell,
Fire, water, earth and air,
Give the world a fright and scare,
Death will come to all who run,
Bodies burnt and skin spun.

Dark underground, dug down deep,
Dark, damp dungeons horribly reek,
Magic words of disgusting choice,
Cackled with a croaky voice.

Hannah Cheung (10)
West Town Lane Junior School, Brislington

Witches' Spells

Disgusting things go in this pot,
Even a jar of runny snot,
Slithering worms, maggot guts,
Newborn children, hair of mutts,
Rabbit intestines, cow dung,
Rat tails, bats' tongues.

Stir it, stir it, stir it round,
You'll know it's ready by the wolf's hound.

Cat ears, frog eyes,
Shark's teeth, old fogey thighs,
Dead mice, horse's hoof,
Rhino guts, snake's tooth,
Snail's shell, rat nails,
Lizard leg, donkey tails.

Stir it, stir it, stir it round,
You'll know it's ready by the wolf's hound.

Skeleton bones, werewolf nose,
Dog's head, eye of crows,
Sheep leg, dragon breath,
If you drink some, it's immediate death.

Bradley Meaker (10)
West Town Lane Junior School, Brislington

The Witches' Pie!

Guts of rat and tail of snail,
Followed by a slug's tail,
Eye of newt, an old fat cat,
Lying on an old mat.
Maggots feeding on dead flies,
Sculling around on a spy.

Double, double, toil and trouble,
Fire burn and cauldron bubble.

An old man's feet
And a filthy old sheet,
Two tonnes of snakes
And old baked cakes.
People who are shy
And someone's thigh.

Double, double, toil and trouble,
Fire burn and cauldron bubble.

A puppy-dog's eye,
A greasy old pie,
A pot of dark pepper
And a black sweater.

Joshua Hughes (10)
West Town Lane Junior School, Brislington

Witches' Potion

Croak of frog, eye of snail
Screech of bat, add a nail
Venom of snake, slime of beer
Breath of cat, diced-up deer
Dead man's toe, fang of bat
Seethed fingers, dirt off mat

Double, double, toil and trouble
Fire burn and cauldron bubble

Bloody hand, scale off dragon
Creepy-crawlies, egg off wagon
Fin of sea shark, bloody goo
Cremated ashes, smelly poo
Mummy's bandage, witches' warts
Troll's bogeys and sweaty shorts

Double, double, toil and trouble
Fire burn and cauldron bubble.

Joshua Woodman (10)
West Town Lane Junior School, Brislington

My Bubbling Cauldron

All blown up in a bubble,
Mixed in well and looks like trouble.

Frogs' legs and lots of guts,
Smelly feet and rotting nuts.
Boil in a baking pan,
Old teeth from my gran.
Pile of bogeys, blob of snot,
Mix in well in a bubbling pot.

All blown up in a bubble,
Mixed in well and looks like trouble.

Toad and cats go really well,
Mix it up and that's my spell.
Stir that in with all the rest,
Then my poison is the best.
Bats that are flying all around,
All the rats running on the ground.
This really looks like fun,
All mixed up and I'll be done!

All blown up in a bubble,
Mixed in well and looks like trouble!

Bethany Newman (10)
West Town Lane Junior School, Brislington

Witches' Poem!

Eye of spider, heart of a rat
Pus of a boil, fang of a bat
Ghost from the past, human blood
Lungs of a dog, old slimy mud
Dead man's hand, blood of night
Flesh of day, a dreadful fright

Double, double, toil and trouble
Fire burn and cauldron bubble

Deadly vomit, leg of dog
Slime of snail, head of a hog
Flesh-eating maggots, brain of ant
Cold, rainy weather, dark witches' chant
Snot-covered phlegm, dead man's eyes
Rotten flesh, bogey pies

Double, double, toil and trouble
Fire burn and cauldron bubble

Wing of a bird, leg of a frog
Blood of a cat, snot of a hog
Pinch up the nose, blood-filled lake
Foot of a duck, vomit cake
Deadly poison, cheesy toes
Scent of a skunk, beak of crows.

Sophie Tatum (10)
West Town Lane Junior School, Brislington

The Witches' Poem

Gut of pig, heart of cat
Blood of cow, hair of rat
Gills of fish, eye of snake
Old school meals, rotting cake
Fire of dragon, skin of bat
Old cabbage, a pile of fat

Double, double, toil and trouble
Fire burn and cauldron bubble

Meat of cow, flesh of seal
Spinach from a watery meal
A wart from an old human man
Rust from a rotten smelly van
A fire that is ablaze
An old rat that's had its days

Double, double, toil and trouble
Fire burn and cauldron bubble

A bit of mischief from Bart
Mouldy crust of an old jam tart
Mix it up in a pair of lungs
Add some spice from slimy tongues
Take it all back in time
To ghosts buried in grime

Double, double, toil and trouble
Fire burn and cauldron bubble.

Kirsty Whatling & Emily Bourne (10)
West Town Lane Junior School, Brislington